PSYCHOLOGY OF EMOTIONS, MOTIVATIONS AND ACTIONS

INTERNET ADDICTION

PSYCHOLOGY OF EMOTIONS, MOTIVATIONS AND ACTIONS

Additional books in this series can be found on Nova's website under the Series tab.

Additional E-books in this series can be found on Nova's website under the E-books tab.

INTERNET THEORY, TECHNOLOGY AND APPLICATIONS

Additional books in this series can be found on Nova's website under the Series tab.

Additional E-books in this series can be found on Nova's website under the E-books tab.

PSYCHOLOGY OF EMOTIONS, MOTIVATIONS AND ACTIONS

INTERNET ADDICTION

HANNAH O. PRICE
EDITOR

Nova Science Publishers, Inc.
New York

For permission to use material from this book please contact us:
Telephone 631-231-7269; Fax 631-231-8175
Web Site: http://www.novapublishers.com

Additional color graphics may be available in the e-book version of this book.

LIBRARY OF CONGRESS CATALOGING-IN-PUBLICATION DATA
Internet addiction / editors, Hannah O. Price.
p. cm.
Includes index.
ISBN 978-1-61122-058-2 (softcover)
1. Internet addiction. 2. Internet--Psychological aspects. I. Price,
Hannah O.
RC569.5.I54I54 2010
616.85'84--dc22
2010037898

Published by Nova Science Publishers, Inc. † New York

CONTENTS

PREFACE

Since the Internet's early widespread use in the mid-1990s, Internet addiction has been identified as a legitimate psychological disorder with significant implications for an individual's cognitive, emotional, and social development. This book presents current research from across the globe in the study of Internet Addiction, including Internet Addiction in adolescence and emerging adulthood; on-line pathological gambling; the Internet and its negative impact on adolescents' sexuality; and the mal-treatment of internet addicts in China.

Chapter 1 - Since the Internet's early widespread use in the mid-1990s, Internet addiction has been identified as a legitimate psychological disorder with significant implications for an individual's cognitive, emotional, and social development (Beard and Wolf, 2001; Greenfield, 1999; Modayil, Thompson, Varnhagen, and Wilson, 2003; Suller, 1999; Young, 2004 and 2006). Extensive literature has accumulated on Internet addition in adolescence and emerging adulthood in the United States and in China (e.g., Chou and Hsiao, 2000; Fortson, Scotti, Chen, Malone, and Del Ben, 2007; Hall and Parsons, 2001; Kandell, 1998; Kubey, Lavin and Barrows, 2001; Li, Wang and Wang, 2009; Lin, Ko and Wu, 2008; Niemz, Griffiths and Banyard, 2005; Wang, 2001; Yang and Zhou, 2005; Zhang, Amos, and McDowell, 2008). Thus, it is important to review these studies and compare Internet addiction among adolescents and college students between the United States and China in an effort to understand the patterns of Internet use in both countries.

Chapter 2 - A plethora of measurement instruments for problematic Internet use (PIU) has been developed. The authors examine their varying factor structures, the factor analytic techniques used to develop these measures, and their implications for factorial validity. They also discuss issues related to how the PIU construct is defined, particularly the lack of definitional independence between the phenomenon and its consequences. The chapter concludes with a summary of the factorial analytic and definitional issues discussed.

Chapter 3 - On-line pathologiocal gambling corresponds to the addictive use of money games on the Internet. It represents a new form of Internet addiction. There is no consensual definition for on-line pathological gambling but pathological gambling in "real life" has one. American Psychiatric Association considers pathological gambling disorder as an Impulse control disorder (American Psychiatric Association, 1994). This behavior is a compulsive and uncontrolled behavior that aims to meet a desire and produces pleasure. The behavior is continued despite the fact that leads to difficulties, and it penetrates deeply into the social life of the patient. On-line pathological gambling thus represents a modern and frequent form of pathological gambling. Online pathological gambling is a new form of addiction. The past decade has witnessed an increased expansion in the types of available gambling activities and their accessibility. Participation in Internet gambling is growing to. For many gamblers, Internet gambling may be an attractive new activity.

Chaper 4 - Aim: to bring to light potential interactions between the use of the Internet, in particular for sexual purposes, and sexual issues during adolescence, whether these be general (psychosomatic, personality, communicational) or specific (sexual orientation, sexual identity, couple). Method: confronting our clinical experience with information found in MEDLINE, PSYCARTICLE, PSYCINFO literature. Results: if numerous studies have been conducted on the Internet's impact on certain aspects of young people's sexuality (misogyny, traumatism, transsexualities,…) none have systemised their approach in function of the psychosexual developmental issues. By rereading and reclassifying these studies concerning their area of impact, if we fear possible consequences on various issues, nothing can allow us today to establish that these are inevitably negative. The most obvious example is when we compare young people's sexuality between those that are looking for sexual partners via the Internet and those that do not, the only differences found are virtual. On the other hand, with regards to young people with an already pre-existing developmental problem, the Internet seems to act as a catalyst aggravating the specific problem. In conclusion: at this moment in time, and considering the small number of studies that have actually been conducted with extremely varying methodologies, nothing allows for the generalisation that the Internet has a negative impact on adolescents' and young adults' sexuality.

Chapter 5 - Although psychology and psychiatry experts around the world continue to debate the nature and definition of internet addiction (IA), there have been widespread efforts to treat youths exhibiting pathological cyber use in China. It is estimated that more than 300 treatment centres have been established throughout China and that they have accumulated a gross income in excess of US$100 million since the mid-2000s. Non-evidence-based therapies, using unscientific and inhumane approaches are, however, pervasive such as the misuse of psychotropic medication, solitary confinement, excessive physical punishment, and involuntary electroconvulsive therapy. The rapid and uncontrolled expansion of IA treatment industry in China is attributable to the country's unique political and socio-economic environment, giving rise to the urgent need to standardize the definition of internet addiction for contemporary public health workers and to develop evidence-based treatments.

Chapter 6 - Internet is one of the major inventions of 20th century. For most users, Internet is at the same time a way of communication, a convivial and powerful workspace and a recreational activity. Internet therefore became essential to the daily lives of more than one billion people [1]. In 1982, the word Internet made its appearance and the web became accessible to the public in the 90's. Its almost unlimited possibilities, in the field of the communication and the diffusion of knowledge, make it a very popular tool. Internet quickly rapidely became essential in the professional sphere as a powerful tool of transferring and sharing data and in the privacy of homes as an essential need to open up to the world and knowledge. A majority of specialists estimates that between 6% and 8% of Internet users would be dependent. Nevertheless, as the phenomenon is still too recent, the national and world prevalence of cyber addiction still seems difficult to quantify [2].

Chapter 7 - The creation of the Internet has had several positive and negative results on the world. Additionally, certain aspects of the Internet make it a unique medium of communication with its own set of norms, standards, language, etc. These various factors have influenced children and adolescents. Problematic Internet use, which has become known as Internet addiction, is not limited by demographic elements. However, there may be certain factors about this medium that could make children and adolescents vulnerable to using the Internet in a dysfunctional way. These factors are examined.

Additionally, special considerations and treatment options are reviewed for mental health professionals who treat children and adolescents for their problematic Internet use. Future research on particular aspects of problematic Internet use with children and adolescents is suggested.

In: Internet Addiction
Editor: Hannah O. Price
ISBN 978-1-61122-058-2

Chapter 1

INTERNET ADDICTION IN ADOLESCENCE AND EMERGING ADULTHOOD: A COMPARISON BETWEEN THE UNITED STATES AND CHINA

Lawrence M. Paska and Zheng Yan
State University of New York at Albany, New York, USA

INTRODUCTION

Since the Internet's early widespread use in the mid-1990s, Internet addiction has been identified as a legitimate psychological disorder with significant implications for an individual's cognitive, emotional, and social development (Beard and Wolf, 2001; Greenfield, 1999; Modayil, Thompson, Varnhagen, and Wilson, 2003; Suller, 1999; Young, 2004 and 2006). Extensive literature has accumulated on Internet addition in adolescence and emerging adulthood in the United States and in China (e.g., Chou and Hsiao, 2000; Fortson, Scotti, Chen, Malone, and Del Ben, 2007; Hall and Parsons, 2001; Kandell, 1998; Kubey, Lavin and Barrows, 2001; Li, Wang and Wang, 2009; Lin, Ko and Wu, 2008; Niemz, Griffiths and Banyard, 2005; Wang, 2001; Yang and Zhou, 2005; Zhang, Amos, and McDowell, 2008). Thus, it is important to review these studies and compare Internet addiction among adolescents and college students between the United States and China in an effort to understand the patterns of Internet use in both countries.

Theoretical and practical significance exists in reviewing the literature on Internet addiction in adolescence and emerging adulthood in the United States and in China. The United States was among the earliest populations to use the Internet, and has encountered Internet addiction since the 1990s (Grohol, 1999; Young, 1998). China has the largest population to use the Internet, and has encountered Internet addiction since the 2000s (Cao and Su, 2006; Chou, 2001; Ko, Yen and Chen, 2009; Li and Chung, 2006). Internet addiction studies in China encompass the mainland, Hong Kong, and Taiwan. Comparing similarities and differences in the prevalence, severity, and social-cultural context of Internet addiction between the two countries provides some unique insights into the investigation and potential treatment of Internet addiction across cultures. It also suggests the need to compare the impact on educational achievement that such addiction has on learners in both countries. In addition, both adolescence and emerging adulthood between the late teens and early twenties (Arnett, 2000) are characterized by a high degree of dynamic life changes. It therefore becomes important to understand the impact and implications of Internet addiction both on adolescents and on those leaving adolescence but not yet fully integrated into adulthood.

This chapter reviews major existing studies of Internet addiction among students in adolescence and emerging adulthood in the United States and in China. It begins by outlining the significance of such a literature review. The main body of the chapter (1) compares the various definitions of Internet addiction among adolescents and emerging adults in both countries; (2) compares the similarities and differences between the prevalence of Internet addiction in both countries; and (3) compares specific addictive behaviors and connects them to the Internet in a socio-cultural context of understanding such addictions. It concludes with a call to further study the effects that Internet addiction has on academic achievement in both countries as a logical and necessary expansion of the current literature.

INTERNET ADDICTION IN THE UNITED STATES AND CHINA

Internet addiction does not have an exact or precise definition between both countries, and is explained and categorized in various ways, along with multiple measures for its diagnosis and treatment. These definitions and measures result from the many new paths that the Internet has forged specifically for social and professional interaction, and generally for human development. In addition to a large variation in defining Internet addiction, research in China also focuses on its treatment. Research in both the United States and China specifically address computer games as a major component of Internet addiction, and focus their attention on addictive behavior resulting from online gaming.

The Internet is simultaneously seen as "a new social environment....a cultural tool kit....a new object of cognition...a gigantic virtual complex network of networks....[and] a new research environment that requires the development of new methodologies" (Greenfield and Yan, 2006, pp. 392-93). As such, the root and spread of Internet addiction takes hold in many different forms and contains many different factors. Unsurprisingly, many terms are used to define or describe the collective phenomenon of Internet addiction. These terms include compulsive Internet use (Caplan, 2005); problematic (Caplan, 2002, 2003 and 2005) or pathological (Lei and Wu, 2007) Internet use, both abbreviated as PIU; pathological computer use (Young, 2009a); Internet behavior dependence (Hall and Parsons, 2001); and, most commonly and generally, Internet addiction (the term used in many of the studies cited in this chapter). Nearly all researchers agree that Internet addiction exists, even if the terms they use to define this addiction differ. One recent push (Block, 2008) is to ensure that Internet addiction is recognized in the forthcoming Diagnostic and Statistical Manual, DSM-V.

An early definition of Internet addiction appeared in the (appropriately named) Internet Addiction Test (Young, 1996). This test was developed to address six potential factors of addiction: salience, excessive use, neglecting work, feelings of heightened anticipation, diminished self-control, and neglecting one's social life. These factors were subsequently correlated to three uses of the Internet (general, personal, and professional) to determine the test's psychometric properties (Widyanto and McMurran, 2004). The proposed criteria for Internet addiction were expanded to include at least one of the following symptoms: risking personal loss, lying to others, or using the Internet for escapism (Beard and Wolf, 2001). Although further test validation was recommended, Young's Internet Addiction Test appeared to list reliable and accepted addiction factors.

Other studies or tests of Internet addiction have been conducted to define Internet addiction in countries outside of the United States and China, such as in the United Kingdom and Canada. In a cognitive-behavioral model of problematic Internet use, "the symptoms are obsessive thoughts about the Internet, diminished impulse control, inability to cease Internet usage, and importantly, feeling that the Internet is an individual's only friend" (Davis, 2001, p. 193; see also Caplan, 2002). Davis described that such individuals, while likely "prone to maladaptive cognitions" from the start (p. 192), would likely have not seen such addictive tendencies play out if not for the existence of the Internet. The author distinguished between both specific and generalized addictions, describing how the cognitive-behavioral model separated pathological use for specific purposes, such as online gaming, compared to more general behaviors such as sending excessive e-mail communications.

On the other hand, many potential signs related to Internet addiction may have developed long before participants' serious use of the Internet (Modayil, Thompson, Varnhagen and Wilson, 2003). In other words, certain addictive tendencies were already present, and manifested themselves in excessive Internet use once the Internet became widely popular as a tool in daily life. One concern of these studies was the self-selected nature of participants: such participants did not likely represent the general population, but were heavy Internet users from the beginning (Modayil, Thompson, Varnhagen and Wilson, 2003; Widyanto and McMurran, 2004). Nevertheless, such heavy Internet users likely already had recognized disorders that manifested themselves in other areas (e.g., alcohol or drug abuse, sexual compulsion, or gambling), so their Internet addiction was one aspect of a larger problem with impulse control (Young, 1996).

The Internet was also theorized to provide some benefits for those with addictive tendencies, as it potentially created more positive social interactions in a new space. Early in the Internet addiction research, Grohol (1999) cautioned that the overuse of technologies like the Internet would, in time, be no different from overuse of other man-made tools such as televisions. "We may be simply observing a temporal-based phenomenon that is due to the unfamiliarity and newness of the technology" (p. 397). From such a perspective, Internet addiction may not be an addiction at all, but merely a symptom of normal human behavior with a new type of technology. It could be taken in perspective with other leisure activities whose overuse leads to general worry and speculation. Grohol further cautioned that the early literature consisted "mainly of exploratory surveys and case studies, which cannot establish relationships between specific behaviors and their causes" (p. 397).

In the United States, Internet addiction has been broadly defined. Suler (1999) initially proposed eight factors that clarified the degree of healthy qualities in Internet activities: "the number and types of needs being addressed by the activity....the underlying degree of deprivation....the type of Internet activity....the effect of Internet activity on in-person level of functioning....subjective feelings of distress....conscious awareness of needs....experience and the phase of involvement....[and] the balance and integration of in-person and cyberspace living" (pp. 386-87). Suler suggested that several needs—including the need for achievement and belonging—contributed to healthy versus unhealthy qualities. The last quality identified was dubbed the "integration principle," in which "Internet use becomes pathological when it is disassociated from in-person life. It becomes healthy when it is integrated with in-person living" – or, reality (p. 393). The degree of Internet addiction was also influenced by a person's age and education. "Changes in the availability and nature of Internet services appear to have eliminated gender and racial gaps [among college students]. Students and homemakers, however, remain particularly susceptible to this disorder" (Hall and Parsons, 2001, p. 315). Ybarra, Alexander and Mitchell (2005) similarly concluded that "youth with major depressive symptomatology are much more likely to talk with strangers online....[and engage in] personal disclosure" (p. 17)--although gender differences reflected "magnitude of associations with depressive symptoms rather than actual types of Internet use" (p. 17). Addiction can be determined by one's use and the content accessed online, and treated with cognitive behavior therapy (Hall and Parsons, 2001).

In addition to defining Internet addiction as a broad research area, several types of Internet addiction have also been identified. Major issues that have been researched to describe aspects of Internet addiction include Internet use and time; identifiable problems related to Internet addiction; gender differences; other psychosocial variables; and attitudes toward computers (Chou, Condron and Belland, 2005). These research areas have differing results. Overall, "only one negative impact [of heavy Internet use] can be identified: time-disruption, leading to interference with academic work, professional performance, daily routines, and so on....impacts of heavy Internet use on addicts' social relationships are inconclusive to positive" (p. 370). Men and women use the Internet in different ways, although men more likely display addictive tendencies. Yet results on psychosocial variables and attitudes toward computers are still inconclusive.

Further research into types of Internet addiction was conducted by Young (2009a), who proposed that pathological computer use consisted of any one of three behavior types: excessive gaming, online sexual preoccupations, and e-mailing or texting. Griffiths (2000) based Internet addiction on the five core components of any addiction: "salience, mood modification, tolerance, withdrawal, conflict and relapse" (p. 211). Based on these competencies, only two of five studied people were considered to have Internet addiction, and these were male teenagers. Others displayed symptoms akin to Internet addiction, but it was hypothesized that excessive Internet use in these individuals addressed deficiencies in other areas, such as lack of friendships. In adolescents, one of the significant predictors of Internet addiction was attention deficit hyperactivity disorder (ADHD), which should be detected early for maximum prevention (Ko, Yen, Chen, 2009). Song, LaRose, Eastin and Lin (2004) dubbed Internet addiction as a new type of gratification, with several factors (such as seeking information, maintaining relationships, and forming a virtual community) being among the gratifications addressed through such addiction by United States college students. In another study, LaRose and Eastin (2004) surveyed general adults in the United States and determined "that media exposure may be predicted from media gratifications....[and that] among newer Internet users...the correlation between expected outcomes and usage were higher than among those with more experience" (pp. 371-372).

In China, definitions of Internet addiction were followed by a focus on treatment, leading to a description of several coping strategies (Zeng, Tan and Zhang, 2006). Based on a study of Taiwanese adolescents, Ko, Yen, Yen, Lin and Yang (2007) recommended that prevention and treatment strategies focus on "high exploratory excitability and low reward dependence...low self-esteem, low family function, and online gaming" as significant risk factors for Internet addiction (p. 550). Middle level students displayed addiction tendencies associated with the family's level of achievement, control, and organization (Li, 2007). In short, structured family environments with high and tightly controlled expectations were seen as possible causes for addiction. On the other hand, Internet addiction was easily curtailed with proper parental monitoring of Internet activities and supervision of children's daily activities, including the frequent encouragement of participation in non-Internet related activities (Lin, Lin and Wu, 2009). When adolescents displayed strong addictive qualities, treatment was possible. The first study of an Internet addiction treatment program for Chinese adolescents suggested that the program was likely effective. The treatment model itself focused on, among many aspects, healthy and safe Internet use, and both individual and family counseling (Shek, Tang and Lo, 2009). Treatment itself was possible since the level of Internet addiction could be significantly predicted by several cognitive factors, including "positive and negative outcome expectancy...[and] refusal self-efficacy of Internet use" (Lin, Ko and Wu, 2008, p. 453). In fact, the authors recommended a specific strategy for emerging adults: "emphasize plans to reduce the positive outcome expectancy of Internet use…and provide information on enhancement skills in refusal self-efficacy of Internet use" (p. 455). In short, it is important to work with emerging adults and help train them to not see Internet use as an unlimited source of good experiences.

A common thread between the research in the United States and China is the understanding that various types of Internet addiction exist among adolescents and emerging adults, and these types will likely increase as the tools, social media sites, games, and virtual environments created to access and enjoy the Internet continue to expand. Two types of Internet-based games for which addiction has been studied include general computer games (see Wan and Chiou, 2007) and massively multiplayer online role-playing games--or MMORPGs (see Smahel, Blinka, and Ledabyl, 2008).

General computer game addiction has been studied frequently in both the United States and China, with similar results about its spread and resulting behaviors. Reward dependence was a strong factor in the excessive use of online games, as Han et al. (2007) concluded in their study of adolescents and the effect on dopamine genes. Some of the many warning signs of online gaming addiction included an intense focus and preoccupation on gaming; lying or hiding one's use of games; a loss of interest in previously-enjoyed hobbies or activities; face-to-face social withdrawal; adoption of defensive or angry positions toward others; psychological withdrawal; use of games as a form of escapism; and continued use despite knowledge of and experience with its consequences, such as missed opportunities (Young, 2009a and b). In a study of "Net-geners" (those between ages 16-24, or the span of mid-adolescence to emerging adulthood), Leung (2004) determined that addiction was prevalent in heavy users who used the Internet for gaming and social networks such as instant messaging and chat rooms, while adolescents were not addicted when their use was largely for information gathering. Interestingly, Net-geners' heavy Internet use signaled a switch in the popular media consumed by adolescents, as addicts watched television significantly less than non-adults. Similar results were even found beyond both countries. For example, in a Canadian study with implications for students in the United States, adolescent males spent more time online and gaming, which resulted positively in stronger personal friendships but negatively in diminished parental relationships (Willoughby, 2008). Interestingly, moderate Internet use had a more positive effect than no Internet use or excessive Internet use.

MMORPGs are of particular interest to scholarship in the United States. Unsurprisingly, the more time that adolescents spend in such environments, the greater likelihood they can develop an Internet addiction. Adolescents are more likely than adults to spend a lot of time with MMORPGs; with such increased intensity of play comes a likelihood of addiction. Adolescents demonstrating Internet addiction were affected by the virtual characters they created. They saw such characters as role models and desiring to become like them in real life (Smahel, Blinka and Ledabyl, 2008). In particular, adolescents who preferred the virtual worlds of games tended to demonstrate psychological dependency on such games, and demonstrated weaknesses in social skills outside of the game (Liu and Peng, 2009). Caplan, Williams and Yee (2009) confirmed these results in their study of problematic Internet use (PIU) among United States college students. PIU was best determined by students who used such games for escapism or immersion, followed by students who used voice technology to connect and bond with other players in the virtual community (p. 1317). Caplan (2005) proposed a model to show that people who lacked self-presentation skills tended to prefer online social interactions, which in turn promoted a more compulsive Internet use, and subsequent addiction.

Adolescents in Taiwan were addicted to online gaming for many of the same reasons as their counterparts in the United States. Wan and Chiou (2006) interviewed ten adolescents and concluded that online gaming satisfied needs for escapism and excitement in their lives. In particular, role-playing games enabled adolescents to take on challenges, character traits, and actions that they would not normally do in real life. The sense of power, authority, and superiority, coupled with a sense of control, mean that online gaming is a serious addiction in China. Wan and Chiou recommended a psychoanalysis approach to treatment. In their two follow-up studies, Wan and Chiou (2007) wrote that Taiwanese adolescents addicted to the Internet displayed higher intrinsic motivation compared to their non-addicted counterparts--also similar to students in the United States. Intrinsic motivation more likely predicted a pathological use of online gaming. Interestingly, "the nonaddicts' extrinsic motivation was significantly higher than their intrinsic motivation," and "four factors (expectancy, relevance, tangibility, and contingency) would moderate extrinsic motivators (such as reward) to undermine intrinsic motivation and function as predicted from the cognitive perspective of human motivation" (p. 190). Intrinsic motivation was also found to be a strong force for motivation and satisfaction.

Emerging adults in China also discussed addictions with the Internet and online gaming. In an early study of gaming and Internet addiction, Chou and Hsaio (2000) reported that Taiwanese college students spent far more time online in games, chat rooms, and using Internet applications than non-addicts, saw the Internet as a source of escapism and fun, but also that it negatively impacted and disrupted their daily routines and appointments, such as classes. Such exploratory studies enabled the early identification of such terms as problematic Internet use, and subsequently Internet addiction, in the collective vocabulary.

Since adolescents lack a strong defined sense of self, treatment for Internet addiction should develop self-esteem and a sense of personal identity independent of the gaming world--and perhaps independent of media in general. If frequent and intense use can be considered overuse but does not result in loss of friendships, employment, sleep, and so forth, is it really an addiction? Griffiths (2010) recommended that gaming Internet addiction should be defined by the extent to which overuse of gaming affects other aspects of a user's life. Over a decade after general Internet addiction was first defined and explained in the United States and China, it remains unclear where the line is drawn between addiction and simply above average use. In the area of online gaming, a specific pattern of overuse has been shown to result in specific consequences for time management and "real-life" interpersonal relationships.

SIMILARITIES AND DIFFERENCES IN INTERNET ADDICTION BETWEEN THE UNITED STATES AND CHINA

Several studies highlight the similarities and differences between both countries in the prevalence of Internet addiction (Grohol, 1999; Cao and Su, 2006; Chou, 2001; Ko, Yen and Chen, 2009; Li and Chung, 2006; Young, 1998; Zhang, Amos, and McDowell, 2008). Case descriptions of Internet addiction are relatively similar between the United States and China; a significant difference between them rests in how adolescents and emerging adults access the Internet. "Unlike in Asia, where Internet cafés are frequently used, in the United States games and virtual sex are accessed from the home" (Block, 2008, p. 306). This factor may also explain the specific prevalence of MMORPGs in the United States, where they can be easily played in the comfort, privacy, and unlimited use of a home computer, without time and expense constraints. Likewise, adolescents in the United States tend to have more private communications with people who are part of their daily lives, and largely focused on basic yet private topics, in their private settings (Gross,

2004). Thus, an accurate picture of Internet addiction in the United States may be difficult to paint.

In China, however, efforts to screen and treat Internet addiction, in addition to setting regulations that prohibit or recommend limits on computer use, make the identification of Internet addiction a bit easier. Chinese policy contrasts with Internet addiction in the United States, which (according to Block, 2008) is often associated with other forms of addiction, and only treated when identified in tandem with such addictions. This practice alone is used to justify the inclusion of Internet addiction in the forthcoming DSM-V manual.

In the United States, the prevalence of Internet addiction is likely easier to identify in college and university settings, where a condition for computer access and use is student acceptance of policies and regulations for safe and responsible Internet usage (Hansen, 2002). Despite such an assumption, Internet addiction was actually found to be "more common among students in China…than among students in the United States who have been exposed to and have used the Internet longer than have their Chinese counterparts….addiction rates are higher in males than in females, regardless of country-of-origin, and that those individuals who spend more continuous hours per day on the Internet are more likely to be Internet addicts" (Zhang, Amos and McDowell, 2008, p. 729). It is unsurprising that more time online results in a greater chance for addiction; males are likely diagnosed for addition at higher rates because they engage in multiple activities online, such as gaming and viewing pornography, that will likely increase their time spent surfing the Net.

Online social interaction is easily available in both countries, especially as Internet connectivity speeds and ease of access increased exponentially. As early as 1999 in the United States, research on college students identified capacity and access as potential issues on the path to addiction. Greenfield (1999) concluded from his study of United States college students that "the potential for Internet addiction may be related to the speed, accessibility, and intensity of the information accessed online" (p. 411), and that as capacity and access increased, so would addiction. Caplan (2003) wrote that the preference for online social interaction among college students in the United States held a significant role in whether such students demonstrated problematic Internet use or outright addiction. Caplan (2005) further employed the cognitive-behavioral theory of problematic Internet use to affirm his previous findings, that "preference for online social interaction was a significant positive predictor of compulsive use….[and] of negative outcomes….participants' preference for online social interaction predicted the degree to which they reported an inability to control impulses" for communicating online (pp. 730-31). Thus, the desire to get online could easily become a compulsion to stay online.

In the United States, college men tended to demonstrate tendencies that would result in Internet addiction (or at least more problematic use) over women. Although men and women used the Internet equally for academic purposes, men were more likely than women to engage in online social interaction, seek out sexual or illegal material, participate in web-based discussion groups, and play games online (Forston, Scotti, Chen, Malone and Del Ben, 2007). In a related study, Lanthier and Windham (2004) found that social use of the Internet was positively associated with the adjustment of college for males only. Internet use predicted the level of college adjustment in both men and women, regardless of the hours spent online. Negative uses of the Internet were likely associated with a poorer adjustment to college in both genders. Surprisingly, the trends seem different among United States adolescents, who were more likely to be female. This is possibly due to the Internet novelty as a social space for young girls, who crave the personal connections and communications that online spaces provide.

In the United States, research has explored how the characteristics of adolescents were more likely predictors of the types of online activities engaged in than addiction tendencies. Leung (2004) reported that "being 'technologically savvy' and having strong principles in 'information right' are more potent factors in predicting online activities for the Net generation than others like 'uninhibited on the Net' and preoccupation with 'adulthood' and being 'confident.' (p. 345). As with college students in the United States, adolescents who demonstrated a willingness to be open on the Internet risked greater tendencies for addiction.

Internet use among college students in China is heavy. Such use is considered to be positive by interviewed students, despite warning signs to the contrary. As referenced previously, studies in China might be more fruitful in part because so much more is known about Internet addiction there. Early in the decade, Chou (2001) found that "the Internet significantly enhanced [students'] self-identification, closer relationships with friends, and bonding with the world. However, eyesight deterioration and sleep deprivation were the major two negative impacts of Internet use. Other problems included poor grades and job performance" (pp. 583-84). By the end of the decade, however, Internet addiction was found to be a severe problem among college students, with significant psychological consequences. Students with identified Internet addiction reported stronger likelihood of depression and anxiety, and that specific factors including "a single-parent family, the age of first exposure to Internet use, the age of the students, city residence, and homesickness" all contributed to Internet addiction (Ni, Yan, Chen and Liu, 2009, p. 327). As the isolated effects of urban life, non-traditional homes, and early exposure to the Internet are all combined, it is little wonder that excessive users reported a number of psychological concerns and issues surrounding their use. The Internet no longer positively affected relationships, because it had itself become institutionalized in a students' daily life, often filling the void left by such other factors.

Chinese adolescents also displayed a number of attitudes about their Internet use that suggested varying levels of addictive tendencies. Results were consistent with findings at the college level, and were perhaps more troubling given that adolescents do not have as much life experience with the Internet, and have not grown into emerging adulthood yet. As with their college-aged counterparts, Chinese adolescents who were Internet addicts spent more time online than non-addicts. Likewise, those who used the Internet to seek social and entertainment gratification tended to display addictive tendencies (Yang and Tung, 2007). Tsai and Lin (2001) surveyed adolescents and determined that the frequency of use tended to predict compulsive behavior, and associated depression should the Internet be restricted. Those who highly valued the Internet tended to need more time to satisfy their desires online, and reported higher levels of anxiety and problems with their families, their schooling, and their overall well-being.

Yet, it may be the message, not the medium, which causes Internet addiction. Taiwanese adolescents used the Internet as the primary method of accessing information, news, social activities, and general knowledge--but the actual addiction rested in how the Internet was used, not in the Internet as a medium in itself (Tsai and Lin, 2003). Chinese adolescents saw the Internet primarily as a tool (Tsai, 2004), meaning that the average adolescent had a practical and responsible view of the Internet (and computer technology more broadly). The role of family has been documented in many studies, thus suggesting that adolescent Internet addiction should be seen as a family concern and treated appropriately in tandem with other addictions. Yen, Yen, Chen, Chen and Ko (2007) discovered that Internet addiction shared several similarities with other types of addictions in families, such as substance abuse, and required a family-based treatment approach. Adolescents in rural communities suffered slightly higher rates of Internet addiction, although with males more addicted than females (Zhang and Chen, 2009).

In fact, with a high correlation between the Internet and other types of addictions that affect families and communities, the socio-cultural context of Internet addiction could likely be seen as similar in both countries and across age groups. Despite more frequent research from China, this context is important to know, since both countries have broadly defined and found factors causing a general Internet addiction.

SOCIO-CULTURAL CONTEXT OF INTERNET ADDICTION

Internet addiction may be best understood as a result of specific behaviors that share similar characteristics to behaviors that result in other forms of human addiction. Chemical addictions to drugs and physical or emotional addictions to human-made tools and resources are logically related. These behaviors exist among adolescents and emerging adults in both countries. By understanding the social-cultural context of Internet addiction in relation to other addictive phenomena in both countries, it is possible to see how similar Internet addiction is to substance abuse addiction (Yen et al., 2008) including alcohol (Ko et al., 2008), along with emotional factors such as shyness (Chak and Leung, 2004) and anxiety (Scealy, Phillips, and Stevenson, 2002). Shyness can be described in similar terms as loneliness, and anxiety can be described in similar terms as depression.

Recent research on Chinese adolescents, for example, supports the notion that Internet addiction and substance abuse are associated. Such association could also result from more severe psychiatric symptoms including obsessive-compulsive tendencies or hostility (Yen et al., 2008). According to Ko et al. (2006), the causal relationship between personality, Internet addiction, and substance abuse could not be fully identified, but two models suggested the distinction between a comorbid and Internet addiction group. "The first model indicates that vulnerable personality characteristics increase the risk of Internet addiction and substance abuse experience….In the second model, personality differences are the result of substance abuse" (p. 892). Similarly, high reward dependence was displayed in a group that had excessive Internet video game play--similar to groups in studies of other addictions (Han et al., 2007). In a study of over two thousand Taiwanese high school students, Ko et al. (2008) also concluded that adolescents suffering from alcohol abuse or Internet addiction "should be evaluated for comorbidity of each other. Besides, Internet addiction should be prevented and intervened with and grouped with other problem behaviors based on problem behavior theory" (p. 575)--a theory that suggests various adolescent behaviors have "the same psychosocial proneness" (p. 571), including environmental and personality factors. This conclusion was also affirmed in Lam, Peng, Mai and Jing (2009). Thus, Internet addiction can be treated in a similar way to other addictions. Ko et al. also discussed that Internet use is more socially accepted than alcohol use by adolescents (p. 575), suggesting that the risks and consequences of Internet abuse may not be as widely known among Chinese adolescents because of the Internet's widespread use and acceptance.

Additional research on Chinese adolescents further supports the notion that Internet addiction must be taken in context with other types of substance abuse. Male Chinese high school students were 50 percent more likely to have Internet addiction; risk factors included "drinking behavior, dissatisfaction with family, and experience of stressful event—[all] stress-related variables" (Lam, Peng, Mai and Jing, 2009, p. 554). These risks are all a part of a turbulent adolescent's life, in which personal stress is often relieved through experimentation and subsequent abuse and addiction of various products or resources. Liu and Peng (2009) also "confirmed the important roles that psychological dependency...and deficient self-regulation...play in the negative consequences associated with MMOG [massively multiplayer online games] playing" (p. 1310), and that those who prefer the virtual to the real world would be psychologically dependent on virtual worlds. Especially among "non-depressed young girls perceiving low family monitoring, having friends with habitual alcohol drinking was another discriminative factor for Internet addiction" (Yen, Ko, Yen, Chang and Cheng, 2009, p. 362).

Studies in China also identified another mitigating factor in determining Internet addiction and substance abuse: the role of siblings in an adolescents' life. According to Yen, Yen, Chen, Chen and Ko (2007), the "habitual alcohol use of siblings significantly predicted Internet addiction and substance abuse experience of adolescents....Sibling alcohol use may be a result of poor family function; however, the habitual alcohol use of a sibling significantly predicted adolescent Internet addiction even after controlling for family function in the multiple regression model" (p. 326). When broken out by age and gender, younger Taiwanese adolescents seemed most affected by the association between family conflict and Internet addiction, although other consistent factors, such as lack of connection to school or geographic isolation in a rural community (Yen, Ko, Yen, Chang and Cheng, 2009). Among urban middle school students, the family environment was the strongest factor in determining Internet addiction (Li, 2007). Thus, the impact of parenting and family on an adolescents' Internet addiction appears to be a significant component of identifying the behaviors associated with one's abuse of the Internet.

Shyness, alienation, and depression are all potential factors in assessing how Internet addiction starts across cultures. By grade 9 in China, adolescents feel a great deal of pressure for high academic achievement. Strong parental relationships--especially with fathers--can predict the likelihood that abuses and addictions would be less common, especially by emerging adolescence. Conversely, "father-adolescent alienation contributed to PIU [problematic Internet use] directly and also indirectly, mediated by leisure services preference, suggesting that children's security in their relationship is related to positive outcomes" (Lei and Wu, 2007, p. 637). Thus, the trust that is built by a strong parent-child bond is a cornerstone in determining whether resources such as the Internet or drugs are used or abused. Lei and Wu used attachment theory to determine that paternal attachment can be a factor in predicting the experience of Internet use in adolescents. As would be a common conclusion among researchers in the United States, Chinese researchers would suggest the importance of a focus on strong family bonds as a strong prevention of many adolescent addictions.

In addition to alienation being a strong predictor of Internet addiction in Chinese studies, other internal personality traits, such as shyness, a sense of loneliness, and depression are also seen as strong predictors of it. Chak and Leung (2004) discussed an association between shyness and likelihood of Internet addiction, and addressed several other interesting results that support the connection between Internet addiction and lack of self-confidence: "the less faith a person has, the firmer belief the person holds in the irresistible power of others, and the higher trust the person places on chance in determining his or her own course of life" (p. 559). Not only were addicted Chinese adolescents spending more time and having more intense sessions online, full-time students were most susceptible "because of free and unlimited access and flexible time schedules" (p. 559). Ko, Yen, Yen, Lin and Yang (2007) examined the factors of Internet addiction among Taiwan's junior high school population, and identified six factors that determined the severity of Internet addiction: "high exploratory excitability, low reward dependence, low self-esteem, low family function, and online game playing" (p. 545). The findings suggested a mixture of extremes--excitability on the one hand, yet low self-esteem on the other—as equal culprits in assessing addiction. Yang and Tung (2007) focused more on more problematic personality traits such as "dependence, shyness, depression and low self-esteem" as all potential indicators of Internet addiction among Chinese adolescents (p. 79).

Less research on socio-cultural context is focused on emerging adults in China. Yang and Tung (2007) discussed how college students used the Internet to form and sustain friendships. Li and Chung (2006) affirmed that the social utility of the Internet made it an attractive feature that led to problems, specifically health problems such as withdrawal, and interpersonal problems such as time management issues. In both cases, it was discussed that the Internet's ability to play a significant role in an emerging adult's social life creates a troubling problem space. Additional research could focus on the changes in personal Internet use during the transition between adolescence and emerging adulthood in China.

In the United States, however, the Internet's social space is often a place of loneliness--similar to the sense of persona alienation expressed in Chinese studies. Undergraduates completing course work requiring Internet use demonstrated that lonely individuals used the Internet more (including e-mail), sought greater emotional support and personal connections online, and reported more satisfying online friendships (Morahan-Martin and Schumacher, 2003). Yet a cycle of loneliness leading to increased Internet use, further isolation, and further loneliness appeared to be a clear issue to address: "lonely individuals go online to fill social voids and emptiness in their life, but their online time creates voids their non-Internet social life and creates other real life problems….the relationship may be bi-directional" (p. 669). Such bi-directionality further signals just how similar to substance abuse a diagnosis of Internet addiction can be. The authors previously identified that males were more likely to overuse the Internet, especially with games and other advanced sites (Morahan-Martin and Schumacher, 2000). In any case, a preference for online versus face-to-face communication and interaction could develop into negative consequences related to excessive Internet use (Caplan, 2003). Not surprisingly, adolescents who do not cope with their loneliness offline struggle to cope any better online. Seepersad (2004) urged an understanding that offline and online coping behaviors were inextricably linked.

On the other extreme of shyness and loneliness is anxiety. For the purposes of comparison, anxiety and the desire to seek new gratifications and sensations ("sensation-seeking") can realistically be considered in tandem. They may also be compared to hyperactivity and other forms of problematic behaviors. A relationship between Internet addiction and sensation-seeking has been identified in China (Shi, Zhou and Ge, 2005). In fact, boys and middle school students were more prone than girls and high school students. Lei and Guo (2008) confirmed the gender and age disparity, and concluded that both separation anxiety and rejection expectancy were positive predictors of problematic Internet use. Among adolescents, males demonstrated a higher association between Internet addiction and frustration intolerance and emotional discomfort (Ko, Yen, Yen, Chen and Wang, 2008).

Chinese adolescents could therefore use the Internet to effectively manage their moods. Leung (2007) found that stress and anxiety from stressful life events were reduced, in large measure, based on the coping strategies and relationships fostered by adolescents while online. Although such managing and coping mechanisms are possible for the well-trained adolescent user, the problem is more severe for elementary-level learners: the level of attention deficit hyperactivity disorder (ADHD) symptoms and Internet addiction were associated with and a strong factor in determining whether young learners were susceptible to Internet addiction (Yoo et al., 2004). By adolescence, ADHD sufferers who go online to find social connections, entertainment, information, or some combination of all three, may see reduced positive behaviors, hyperactivity, and even increased likelihood of neuroses and psychoses (Cao and Su, 2006). Unchecked at a early age, disorders such as ADHD could expand and manifest more significant cognitive and social difficulties by emerging adulthood.

The Internet reportedly strengthened peer relations by those adolescents who were both addicted and non-addicted to it. Yet those who were highly dependent on the Internet reported a decreased academic performance and parental relationships (Lin and Tsai, 2002). "Excessive Internet use among Taiwanese high school adolescents may reflect their motivation to strive for personal identity through breaking social inhibition" (p. 423). The desire for independence and autonomy may lead to addictive tendencies.

Again, by the time of college, emerging adults in China appear to grapple with balancing their understanding of the Internet and its addictive potential. Such students emerge from a personal struggle more likely aware of the power for the Internet to foster strong peer networks. Such networks and relationships come at a cost, and the price is both physical and emotional. College students reported that the Internet created a more positive sense of self and connection to friends and the larger world. "However, eyesight deterioration and sleep deprivation were the major two negative impacts of Internet use....About one-third said they experienced loss, moodiness, anxiety, etc., when they could not log onto the Internet. Some subjects had tried the abstinence methods, which did not often work out" (Chou, 2001, pp. 583-84). Most students did not see their problem as large enough to warrant treatment or counseling. Yet, depression and anxiety were both rated higher in students with Internet addiction. "Students who came from a single-parent family, who were nonresidents of the city where the university is located, who came from cities, or who surfed the Internet more than 4 hours a day had a higher probability of Internet addiction" (Ni, Yan, Chen and Liu, 2009, p. 328). In short, the greater number of factors of geographic and social isolation, the increased likelihood that Internet addiction would occur among Chinese emerging adults. Certainly, if frequent time online provides satisfaction--especially in the opportunities for increased pleasure through communication (Chou and Hsaio, 2000)--then additional supports to help transition emerging adults to college are needed.

The cognitive affects of Internet addiction have also been studied in China. Among college students, those with problematic Internet use chose more negative words on a cognitive test, although all students chose positive words as a sign of their desire to be happy and avoid pain (Zheng, 2009). One striking study showed that emerging adults in China with Internet addiction likely had stronger decision making abilities that those suffering from substance or gambling abuses (Ko, Hsiao, Liu, Yen, Yang and Yen, 2010). The authors hypothesized that "heavy Internet use is usually linked to positive emotional experiences (for example, success in gaming), which might result in not only a positive implicit emotional bias, but also long-term negative consequences when the person loses control. Then, the positive somatic marker for Internet use will become important. This might lead to persistent Internet use" (p. 124). Internet addicts overall have far more "negative processing biases" (Zhi, Qi, Dajun, 2008, p. 352) compared to non-addicts, suggesting a need for further study in the cognitive affects of Internet addiction.

In the United States, sensation-seeking was found to increase in early adolescence but decrease by emerging adulthood, with impulsivity in online spaces decreasing steadily through adolescence (Steinberg and Albert et al., 2008). If curbed appropriately, risky online behaviors can be prevented or controlled earlier through education and counseling. This is especially important because negative outcomes were predicted as an influence of compulsive Internet use (Caplan, 2005), so early detection and education would increase a young learner's ability to work and play responsibly online.

College students in the United States have been the focus of more extensive research on anxiety and related psychological issues surrounding Internet addiction. Social anxiety was found to be a stronger predictor of Internet addiction than loneliness, largely as it "represents a more theoretically powerful predictor in that it provides a clear motivation for why some people might prefer the altered interpersonal context available in CMC [computer-mediated communication" (Caplan, 2007, p. 240). In the context of online gaming, however, loneliness seems to play a larger role. According to Caplan, Williams and Yee (2009), "loneliness, introversion, aggression, addiction, and depression were significant predictors of PIU [problematic Internet use] and that loneliness was the single most influential predictor in the model. Interestingly, a previous diagnosis of anxiety disorder was not a significant predictor" (p. 1318). Both studies affirmed that one's desire for online social interaction was a more positive predictor of Internet addiction.

Among college students, depression in general also appeared to be the largest reason for Internet addiction (Fortson, Scotti, Chen, Malone and Del Ben, 2007). Depression again resulted from a desire to meet people online and to participate in fewer face-to-face interactions. Although loneliness was not specifically addressed, clearly such fears as social anxiety manifest themselves in a desire to socialize predominantly in an anonymous fashion. Liu and Peng (2009) studied those just exiting emerging adulthood (in their mid-twenties) and proposed that online social interaction may be a way to satisfy deficient social skills, thus favoring a virtual world for gaming and interpersonal relations. However, loneliness and depression were not found to influence a preference for virtual life. Perhaps as learners get older, their desires to be online and tendencies toward Internet addiction are less about loneliness and anxiety and more about general incompetent social skills--a lifetime of poorly developed habits in the ability to relate to others and form lasting interpersonal connections. Overall, loneliness, shyness, anxiety, depression, and generally poor social skills may contribute to a decrease in educational achievement. By the time young learners have reached full adulthood, their learning may have been impacted due to their Internet addiction caused by a number of interrelated factors. The impact of such addiction on one's ability to handle the emotional, professional, and social needs and responsibilities of adult life rests largely on the strength and quality of the total educational experience.

Educational Implications of Internet Addiction

Future research should further study the educational implications of Internet addiction among adolescents and emerging adults, with a sharp focus on the effects that Internet addiction has on academic achievement in both countries. Academic achievement is one of the most relevant consequences of Internet addiction on adolescents and emerging adults. This recommendation is not new, nor is it isolated to the United States and China. Griffiths, Miller, Gillespie and Sparrow (1999) advocated over a decade ago for a research agenda to understand the implications of the newly recognized Internet addiction on student achievement and learning. At the time, however, the call for such research was to understand the prevalence of Internet addiction and the types of online activities that led to such addiction. A few years later, Griffiths (2001) described that "some of the problems are not from the...medium itself but from what children can do in that medium (e.g. access pornography)" (p. 28). The recommendation was to balance the educational uses of information technology such as the Internet with other (and more traditional) learning tools. The author conceded that teachers should focus on "not what to learn but how to learn" (p. 28). Part of the problem was seen as the understanding that Internet addiction research "has been composed mainly of exploratory surveys and case studies, which cannot establish relationships between specific behaviors and their causes" (Grohol, 1999, p. 397). For the most part, this assertion holds true in 2010 as it did in 2000.

Fully into the 21st century, it is important to seriously understand how learning achievement is affected by Internet use. Among Chinese adolescents, "both the level of IM [instant messaging] use and level of IM addiction have significant and positive bivariate correlations with academic performance decrement. These findings suggest that teenagers' IM use affected their academic performance" (Huang and Leung, 2009, p. 678). By emerging adulthood, Chinese college students demonstrated a higher likelihood of learning burnout when they displayed Internet addiction tendencies (Wei, Yang and Yu, 2007). The greater prevalence of Internet addiction research in China does not mean that such addiction and its implications for learning are completely known. The focus has remained on the students, but not the impact on their learning.

In the United States, some limited research addressed student computer use at home, with word processing and basic research being the primary applications for educational use. An early synthesis of research by Subrahmanyam, Greenfield, Kraut and Gross (2001) suggested that "studies provide preliminary evidence that computer use is positively correlated with academic achievement, but fails to clarify this relationship" (p. 16), further blurring the line between use, overuse, and outright addiction. Indications suggested that the situation had not changed much by mid-decade. Chou, Condron and Belland (2005) reviewed the literature and concluded, "attention should be focused on the inappropriate and indecent use of the Internet and its impacts on youngsters' psychological and physical development" (p. 385). The authors do not go on to suggest a need to consider the attention as it relates to educational achievement. One has to step outside of the United

States and China to find a more definitive correlation between academic achievement and Internet addiction. In a Canadian study, moderate Internet use "was associated with a more positive academic orientation than nonuse and high levels of use....adolescents who do not use the Internet for learning tasks, as well as excessive users of the Internet, are at a disadvantage academically" (Willoughby, 2008, p. 202).

In tandem with a call for research on the educational implications of known and perceived Internet addiction is a call for strong research methods in online environments. It becomes important both to assess and measure the effects of addiction on achievement, and to understand how the Internet itself is a new space in which research is conducted. Greenfield and Yan (2006) proposed that, in order to utilize new online environments "such as chat rooms and bulletin boards, with their unique virtual characteristics, we need to develop new techniques for collecting and analyzing data" (p. 393). Such techniques include how to collect and analyze data directly from the Internet. These techniques relate to how researchers determine the identity of the population sampled, and how they build stronger case studies and experimental studies that provide more conclusive evidence to expand upon the earlier exploratory studies.

In conclusion, Internet addiction exists in adolescents and emerging adults in both the United States and in China. It has distinguishing characteristics--not unlike drug addiction--and manifests itself in multiple environments such as games and chat rooms. Certain personality types are more susceptible to Internet addiction than others, include those who are shy, anxious, depressed, or seek sensation and gratification through their Internet use. Now that the causes and symptoms of Internet addiction have been substantially documented and verified in the literature and research, it is time to understand just how serious this type of addiction is on the educational achievement of a population still progressing through school.

REFERENCES

Arnett, J. J. (2000). Emerging adulthood: A theory of development from the late teens through the twenties. *American Psychologist, 53,* 469-480.

Beard, K. W. and Wolf, E. M. (2001). Modification in the proposed diagnostic criteria for Internet addiction. *CyberPsychology and Behavior, 4,* 377-383.

Block, J. J. (2008). Issues for DSM-V: Internet addiction. *American Journal of Psychiatry, 165*(3), 306.

Cao, F., and Su, L. (2006). Internet addiction among Chinese adolescents: Prevalence and psychological factors. *Child: Care, health and development, 33*(3), 275-281.

Caplan, S. E. (2002). Problematic Internet use and psychosocial well-being: development of a theory-based cognitive-behavioral measurement instrument. *Computers in Human Behavior, 18*, 553-575.

------. (2003). Preference for online social interaction: a theory of problematic Internet use and psychosocial well-being. *Communication Research, 30,* 625 648.

------. (2005). A social skill account of problematic Internet use. *Journal of Communication, 12*, 721-736.

------. (2007). Relations among loneliness, social anxiety, and problematic Internet use. *CyberPsychology and Behavior, 10*, 234-241.

Caplan, S., Williams, D., and Yee, N. (2009). Problematic Internet use and psychosocial well-being among MMO players. *Computers in Human Behavior, 25,* 1312-1319.

Chak, K., and Leung, L. (2004). Shyness and locus of control as predictors of Internet addiction and Internet use. *CyberPsychology and Behavior, 7*(5), 559-570.

Chou, C. (2001). Internet abuse and addiction among Taiwan college students: An online interview study. *CyberPsychology and Behavior,* 4(5), 573–585.

Chou, C., Condron, L, and Belland, J. (2005). A review of the research on internet addiction. *Educational Psychology Review, 17*(4), 363-388.

Chou, C., and Hsiao, M. C. (2000). Internet addiction, usage, gratifications, and pleasure experience-the Taiwan college students' case. *Computer and Education. 35*(1), 65-80.

Davis, R. A. (2001). A cognitive–behavioral model of pathological internet use. *Computers in Human Behavior, 77*, 187–195.

Fortson, B. L., Scotti, J. R., Chen, Y., Malone, J., and Del Ben, K. S. (2007). Internet use, abuse, and dependence among students at a southeastern regional university. *Journal of American College Health, 56*(2), 137-144.

Greenfield, D. N. (1999). Psychological characteristics of compulsive internet use: A preliminary analysis. *CyberPsychology and Behavior, 2*(5), 403–412.

Greenfield, P., and Yan, Z. (2006). Children, adolescents, and the Internet: A new field of inquiry in developmental psychology. *Developmental Psychology, 42,* 391-394.

Griffiths, M., Miller, H., Gillespie, T., and Sparrow, P. (1999). Internet usage and internet addiction in students and its implications for learning. *Journal of Computer Assisted Learning, 15*(1), 85-90.

Griffiths, M. D. (2000). Does Internet and computer "addiction" exist? Some case study evidence. *CyberPsychology and Behavior, 3*(2), 211–218.

-----. (2001). Excessive internet and computer use: Implications for education. *Education and Health, 19*(2), 23-29.

------. (2010). The role of context in online gaming excess and addiction: Some case study evidence. *International Journal of Mental Health and Addiction, 8*(1), 119-125.

Grohol, J. M. (1999). Too much time online: Internet addiction or healthy social interaction? *Cyberpsychology and Behavior, 2*(5), 395-401.

Gross, E. F. (2004). Adolescent Internet use: What we expect, what teens report. *Journal of Applied Developmental Psychology, 25,* 633-649.

Guan, S. S., and Subrahmanyam, K. (2009). Youth Internet use: Risks and opportunities. *Current Opinion in Psychiatry, 22,* 351-356.

Hall, A. and Parsons, J. (2001). Internet addiction: College student case study using best practices in cognitive behavior therapy. *Journal of Mental Health Counseling, 23*(4), 312-327.

Han, D. H., Lee, Y. S., Yang, K. C., Kim, E. Y., Lyoo, I. K., and Renshaw, P. F. (2007). Dopamine genes and reward dependence in adolescents with excessive Internet video game play. *Journal of Addiction Medicine, 1*(3), 133- 138.

Hansen, S. (2002). Excessive Internet usage or 'Internet' addiction?: The implications of diagnostic categories for student users. *Journal of Computer Assisted Learning, 18,* 232-236.

Huang, H., and Leung, L. (2009). Instant messaging addiction among teenagers in China: Shyness, alienation, and academic performance decrement. *CyberPsychology and Behavior, 12*(6), 675-679.

Kandell, J. J. (1998). Internet addiction on campus: The vulnerability of college students. *CyberPsychology and Behavior, 1*(1), 11-17.

Ko, C. H., Hsiao, S., Liu, G. C., Yen, J. Y., Yang, M. J., and Yen, C. F. (2010). The characteristics of decision making, potential to take risks, and personality of college students with Internet addiction. *Psychiatry Research, 175,* 121-125.

Ko, C., Yen, J., Chen, C., Chen, S., Wu, K., and Yen, C. (2006). Tridimensional personality of adolescents with Internet addiction and substance use experience. *Canadian Journal of Psychiatry, 51,* 887-894.

Ko, C., Yen, J., Yen, C., Chen, C., Wang, S. (2008). The association between Internet addiction and belief of frustration intolerance: The gender difference. *CyberPsychology and Behavior, 11*(3), 273-278.

Ko, C., Yen, J., Yen, C., Chen, C., Weng, C., Chen, C. (2008). The association between Internet addiction and problematic alcohol use in adolescents: The problem behavior model. *CyberPsychology and Behavior, 11*(5), 571-576.

Ko, C. H., Yen, J. Y., Chen, C. S. (2009). Predictive values of psychiatric symptoms for Internet addiction in adolescents. *Archives of Pediatric and Adolescent Medicine, 163*(10), 937-943.

Ko, C., Yen, J., Yen, C., Lin, H., and Yang, M. (2007). Factors predictive for incidence and remission of Internet addiction in young adolescents: A prospective study. *CyberPsychology and Behavior, 10,* 545-551.

Kubey, R., Lavin, M., and Barrows, J. (2001). Internet use and collegiate academic performance decrements: Early findings. *Journal of Communication, 51*(2), 366-382.

Lam, L. T., Peng, Z., Mai, J., and Jing, J. (2009). Factors associated with Internet addiction among adolescents. *CyberPsychology and Behavior, 12*(5), 551-555.

Lanthier, R. P., and Windham, R. C. (2004). Internet use and college adjustment: the moderating role of gender. *Computers in Human Behavior, 20,* 591-606.

LaRose, R., and Eastin, M. S. (2004). A social cognitive theory of Internet uses and gratifications: Toward a new model of media attendance. *Journal of Broadcasting and Electronic Media, 48,* 358-377.

Lei, L., and Guo, F. (2008). The relations of adolescents' separation-individuation, the Internet recreation service preference and their pathological Internet use. *Acta Psychologica Sinica, 40*(9), 1021-1029.

Lei, L., and Wu, Y. (2007). Adolescents' paternal attachment and Internet use. *CyberPsychology and Behavior, 10*(5), 633-639.

Leung, L. (2004). Net-generation attributes and seductive properties of the internet as predictors of online activities and internet addiction. *CyberPsychology and Behavior, 7*(3), 333-348.

-----. (2007). Stressful life events, motives for Internet use, and social support among digital kids. *CyberPsychology and Behavior, 10,* 204-214.

Li, H., Wang, J., and Wang, L. (2009). A survey on the generalized problematic Internet use in Chinese college students and its relations to stressful life events and coping style. *International Journal of Mental Health and Addiction, 7,* 333-346.

Li, S. M., and Chung, T. M. (2006). Internet function and Internet addictive behavior. *Computers in Human Behavior, 22*, 1067-1071.

Li, Y. Z. (2007). Internet addiction and family achievement, control, organization. *Chinese Mental Health Journal, 21*(4), 244-246.

Lin, C., Lin, S., and Wu, C. (2009). The effects of parental monitoring and leisure boredom on adolescents' Internet addiction. *Adolescence, 44*(176), 993-1004.

Lin, M. P., Ko, H. C., and Wu, J. Y. W. (2008). The role of positive/negative outcome expectancy and refusal self-efficacy of Internet use on Internet addiction among college students in Taiwan. *CyberPsychology and Behavior, 11*(4), 451-457.

Lin, S. S. J., and Tsai, C. C. (2002). Sensation seeking and Internet dependence of Taiwanese high school adolescents. *Computers in Human Behavior, 18,* 411-426.

Liu, M., and Peng, W. (2009). Cognitive and psychological predictors of the negative outcomes associated with playing MMOGs (massively multiplayer online games). *Computers in Human Behavior,*

Modayil, M. V., Thompson, A. H., Varnhagen, S., and Wilson, D. R. (2003). Internet users' prior psychological and social difficulties. *CyberPsychology and Behavior, 6*(6), 585-590.

Morahan-Martin, J. M., and Schumacher, P. (2000). Incidence and correlates of pathological Internet use. *Computers in Human Behavior, 16*, 13-29.

------. (2003). Loneliness and social uses of the Internet. *Computers in Human Behavior, 19*, 659-671.

Ni, X., Yan, H., Chen, S., and Liu, Z. (2009). Factors influencing Internet addiction in a sample of freshmen university students in China. *CyberPsychology and Behavior, 12*(3), 327-330.

Niemz, K., Griffiths , M., and Banyard, P. (2005). Prevalence of pathological Internet use among university students and correlations with self-esteem, the General health questionnaire (GHQ), and Disinhibition. *CyberPsychology and Behavior, 8*(6), 562-570.

Scealy, M., Phillips, J. G. and Stevenson, R. (2002). Shyness and anxiety as predictors of patterns of Internet usage. *CyberPsychology and Behavior, 5*(6), 507-515.

Seepersad, S. (2004). Coping with loneliness: Adolescent online and offline behavior. *CyberPsychology and Behavior, 7*(1), 35-39.

Shek, D. T. L., Tang, V. M. Y., and Lo, C. Y. (2009). Evaluation of an Internet addiction treatment program for Chinese adolescents in Hong Kong. *Adolescence, 44*(174), 359-373.

Shi, Q., Zhou, R., Ge, Y., Qin, X., and Zhang, K. (2005). Internet addiction disorder and sensation seeking of middle school and high school students. *Chinese Mental Health Journal, 19,* 453-456.

Smahel, D., Blinka, L., and Ledabyl, O. (2008). Playing MMORPGs: Connections between addiction and identifying with a character. *CyberPsychology and Behavior, 11*(6), 715-718.

Song, I., Larose, R., Eastin, M. S., and Lin, C. A. (2004). Internet gratifications and Internet addiction-on the uses and abuses of new media. *CyberPsychology and Behavior, 7*(4), 384-394.

Steinberg, L., Albert, D., Cauffman, E., Banich, M., Graham, S., and Woolard, J. (2008). Age differences in sensation seeking and impulsivity as indexed by behavior and self-report: Evidence for a dual systems model. *Developmental Psychology, 44,* 1764-1778.

Subrahmanyam, K., Greenfield, P., Kraut, R., and Gross, E. (2001). The impact of\ computer use on children's and adolescents' development. *Journal of Applied Developmental Psychology, 22*, 7-30.

Suler, J. R. (1999). To get what you need: healthy and pathological Internet use. *CyberPsychology and Behavior, 2*(5), 355-393.

Suler, J. (2004). Computer and cyberspace addiction. *International Journal of Applied Psychoanalytic Studies, 1*, 359-362.

Tsai, C. C. (2004). Adolescents' perceptions toward the Internet: A 4-T framework. *CyberPsychology and Behavior, 7*(4), 458-463.

Tsai, C. C., and Lin, S. S. J. (2001). Analysis of attitudes toward computer networks and Internet addiction of Taiwanese adolescents. *CyberPsychology and Behavior, 4*, 373-376.

------. (2003). Internet addiction of adolescents in Taiwan: an interview study. *CyberPsychology and Behavior, 4*, 649-652.

Wan, C. J., and Chiou, W. B. (2006). Why are adolescents addicted to online gaming?: An interview study in Taiwan. *CyberPsychology and Behavior, 9*(6), 762-766.

------. (2007). The motivations of adolescents who are addicted to online games: A cognitive perspective. *Adolescence, 42*(165), 179-197.

Wang, W. (2001). Internet dependency and psychosocial maturity among college students. *International Journal of Human-Computer Studies, 55,* 919-938.

Wei, P., Yang, S., and Yu, H.-B. (2007). Relationship between Internet addiction disorder and learning burnout of college students. *Chinese Journal of Clinical Psychology, 15*(6), 650-651.

Widyanto, L., McMurran, M. (2004). The psychometric properties of the internet addiction test. *CyberPsychology and Behavior, 7*(4), 443-450.

Willoughby, T. (2008). A short-term longitudinal study of internet and computer game use by adolescent boys and girls: Prevalence, frequency of use, and psychosocial predictors. *Developmental Psychology, 44,* 195-204.

Yang, S.,C. and Tung, C. J. (2007). Comparison of Internet addicts and non addicts in Taiwanese high school. *Computers in Human Behavior, 23,* 79-96.

Yang, W., and Zhou, Z. (2005). On different types of the personality traits of sensation seeking of college students who have Internet addiction. *Journal of Higher Education, 26*(6), 69-73.

Ybarra, M. L., Alexander, M. P. H., and Mitchell, K. J. (2005). Depressive symptomatology, youth Internet use, and online interactions: A national survey. *Journal of Adolescent Health, 36*, 9-18.

Yen, J., Ko, C., Yen, C., Chen, S., Chung, W., and Chen, C. (2008). Psychiatric symptoms in adolescents with Internet addiction: Comparison with substance abuse. *Psychiatry and Clinical Neurosciences, 62,* 9-16.

Yen, C., Ko, C., Yen, J.., Chang, Y., and Cheng, C. (2009). Multi-dimensional discriminative factors for Internet addiction among adolescents regarding gender and age. *Psychiatry and Clinical Neurosciences, 63,* 357-364.

Yen, J., Yen, C., Chen, C., Chen, S., and Ko, C. (2007). Family factors of Internet addiction and substance use experience in Taiwanese adolescents. *CyberPsychology and Behavior, 10,* 323-329.

Yoo, H., Cho, S., Ha, J., Yune, S., Kim, S., Hwang, J., Chung, A., Sung, Y., and Lyoo, I. (2004). Attention deficit hyperactivity symptoms and Internet addiction. *Psychiatry and Clinical Neurosciences, 58,* 487-494.

Young, K. (1996). Internet addiction: The emergence of a new clinical disorder. *CyberPsychology and Behavior, 3,* 237-244.

------. (2004). Internet addiction: A new clinical phenomenon and its consequences. *American Behavioral Scientist, 48*(4), 402-415.

------. (2009a). Internet addiction: Diagnosis and treatment considerations. *Journal of Contemporary Psychotherapy, 39*, 241-246.

------. (2009b). Understanding online gaming addiction and treatment issues for adolescents. *The American Journal of Family Therapy, 37,* 355-372.

------. (1998). Internet addiction: The emergence of a new clinical disorder. *CyberPsychology and Behavior, 1*(3), 237–244.

Zeng, X. Y., Tan, H. Z., and Zhang, J. Q. (2006). Internet addiction and coping styles in adolescents. *Chinese Journal of Clinical Psychology, 14*(3), 256-257.

Zhang, H., and Chen, L. (2009). A research on the Internet addiction of rural and urban minors and its attribution. *Psychological Science, 32*(3), 748-750.

Zhang, L., Amos, C., and McDowell, W. C. (2008). A comparative study of Internet addiction between the United States and China. *Cyberpsychology and Behavior, 11*(6), 727-729.

Zheng, X. F. (2009). The cognitive characteristics of pathological Internet users in different emotional modes. *Acta Psychologica Sinica, 41*(7), 630-638.

Zhi, W., Qi, J., and Dajun, Z. (2008). An experimental study on the priming affects of Internet addicts. *Psychological Science, 31*(2), 350-355.

In: Internet Addiction
Editor: Hannah O. Price

ISBN 978-1-61122-058-2

Chapter 2

PIU Construct Development: Factorial Analytic and Definitional Issues

Ronnie Jia[1,a] ***and Heather H. Jia***[2,b]
[1] Southern Illinois University, Carbondale, Illinois 62901, USA
[2] Eastern Illinois University, Charleston, Illinois 61920, USA

Abstract

A plethora of measurement instruments for problematic Internet use (PIU) has been developed. We examine their varying factor structures, the factor analytic techniques used to develop these measures, and their implications for factorial validity. We also discuss issues related to how the PIU construct is defined, particularly the lack of definitional independence between the phenomenon and its consequences. The chapter concludes with a summary of the factorial analytic and definitional issues discussed.

[a] ronnie@siu.edu.
[b] hhjia@eiu.edu.

INTRODUCTION

Recent research has documented varying types and degrees of problematic Internet use (PIU). Though different labels have been used to describe the phenomenon – Internet addiction (Young, 1996), Internet dependency (Scherer, 1997), pathological Internet use (Morahan-Martin and Schumacher, 2000), and problematic Internet use (Davis, 2001, Davis, Flett and Besser, 2002) – there emerges cumulative work in this area over the nature of the phenomenon, its various manifestations, as well as psychological and occupational consequences (e.g., Beard and Wolf, 2001; Brenner, 1997; Chou, 2001; Chou, Condron and Belland, 2005; Davis, 2001; Davis et al., 2002; Kraut et al., 1998; Nalwa and Anand, 2003; Treuer, Fabian and Furedi, 2001; Whang, Lee and Chang, 2003; Widyanto and McMurran, 2004; Young, 1996).

A plethora of PIU measurement instruments has been developed. Our literature search has identified a total of 13 scales published in English-language outlets as of 2009. As summarized in Table 1, factorial complexity of these measures varies widely, ranging from single-factor to as complex as seven, which prompts the question: Why does the PIU factor structure vary so much across these measures? What is the true factor structure of PIU?

There are at least two causes for such diverse factor structures for the PIU construct. One is methodological in nature, in that the factor analytic techniques and decision heuristics used in developing these scales can have a direct impact on the factor structure obtained. For example, certain frequently used statistical crteria in factor analysis are known to lead to significant overfactoring (Frazier and Youngstrom, 2007).

The other cause is conceptual in nature – the PIU construct itself has not been uniformly defined across studies, and many existing definitions have conceptual issues. Though there has been some attempts at theory building (e.g., Davis, 2001), there is still a lack of commonly adopted construct definition or theoretical view. Achieving a consensus definition is a critical step before its true factor structure can be discovered because the defnition would determine the domain of the construct and the content of the item pool (Tobacyk, 1995).

These two issues are not entirely independent of each other because scale development and validation is inherently a process driven by theoretical/conceptual as well as empirical considerations. Rigorous methodological approaches can in turn inform our effort toward a consensus definition. If methodological issues are not addressed, more PIU scales of diverse factor structures are likely to be developed in future research even after the adoption of a consensus definition, making it difficult to build a cumulative tradition in this literature.

If the methodological issues can be largely resolved once researchers adopt common, rigorous statistical techniques, conceptual/theoretical advances require much more cumulative research in this nascent area where much work is still descriptive in nature and when closely related reference areas, such as pathological gambling, are in "conceptual chaos" (Shaffer, 1997). As an initial effort toward this direction, our focus on the conceptual front will be on some of the definitional issues with the PIU construct.

In the rest of the chapter, we will discuss these methodological and definitional issues in turn. We begin by reviewing the factor analytic issues in the development of the existing PIU measures and exploring their implications to factorial validity.

Factor Analytic Techniques Employed

Table 1 summarizes the main characteristics of the 13 PIU measures, such as factor structures, validation techniques used and results reported. Three types of factor analytic techniques have been employed in the development of these measures: principal components analysis (PCA), exploratory factor analysis (EFA), and confirmatory factor analysis (CFA). Next, we review these methods and their implications for scale development. We begin with the two exploratory techniques: PCA and EFA.

PCA and EFA

Though both PCA and EFA summarize the relationships between sets of measured variables, letting the data drive the analysis, the two techniques are conceptually and mathematically distinct (Frazier and Youngstrom, 2007). PCA is used to combine measured variables into a small number of principle components, which are simply linear combinations of the original measured variables, rather than latent factors. Since no distinction is made between common and unique sources of variance in the measured variables, PCA has been described as strictly a data reduction technique (Frazier and Youngstrom, 2007).

Table 1. Existing PIU Measurement Instruments

Author	Instrument	Primary Base	Scale Length	Factors	Validation Technique	Factor Loading	Inter-factor Correlation
Young (1998)	Internet Addiction Test (IAT)	DSM-IV	20	Unidimensional	Not Reported	Not Reported	Not Applicable
Davis et al. (2002)	Online Cognition Scale (OCS)	Davis' (2001) cognitive-behavioral model	36	Diminished impulsive control Loneliness/depression Social comfort Distraction	CFA	Reported	Reported
Caplan (2002)	Generalized Problematic Internet Use Scale (GPIUS)	Davis' (2001) cognitive-behavioral model	29	Mood alteration Perceived social benefits Negative outcomes Compulsive use Excessive time online Withdrawal Perceived social control	EFA	Not Reported	Reported (all < .60)
Lin and Tsai (2002)	Internet Addiction Scale for Taiwanese High School Students (IAST)	Prior literature on diagnostic criteria for Internet addiction	29	Tolerance Compulsive use Withdrawal Related problems – family, school and health Related problems – interpersonal and financial	PCA	Not Reported	Not Reported
Pratarelli and Browne (2002)	Internet Use and Addiction	Prior literature	74	Addiction factor Sex factor User factor	EFA and CFA	Reported	Reported
Nichols and Nicki (2004)	Internet Addiction Scale	DSM-IV and other literature	31	Unidimensional	PCA	Not Reported	Not Applicable

Author	Instrument	Primary Base	Scale Length	Factors	Validation Technique	Factor Loading	Inter-factor Correlation
Thathcher and Goolam (2005)	Problematic Internet Usage Questionnaire (PIUQ)	Young's (1996) Internet addiction criteria and other literature	20	Online preoccupation Adverse effects Social interactions	PCA	Reported	Reported (all < .63)
Huang et al. (2007)	Chinese Internet Addiction Inventory (CIAI)	Young's (1998) Internet Addition Test	31	Conflict Mood modification Dependence	EFA and CFA	Reported	Reported (all < .70)
Ceyhan et al. (2007)	Problematic Internet Usage Scale (PIUS)	Expert opinions	33	Negative consequences Social benefit/social comfort Excessive use	PCA	Not Reported	Not Reported
Chang and Law (2008)	The Reivsed Internet Addiction Test (IAT)	Young's (1998) Internet Addiction Test	18	Withdrawal and social problems Time management and performance Reality substitute	PCA and CFA	Reported	Reported (.83, .88, .88)
Demetrovics et al. (2008)	Problematic Internet Use Questionnaire	Young's (1998) Internet Addiction Test and other literature	18	Obssession Neglect Control disorder	PCA	Reported	Reported (all < .52)
Meerkerk et al. (2009)	Compulsive Internet Use Scale (CIUS)	DSM-IV and other literature	14	Unidimensional	CFA	Reported	Not Applicable
Jia and Jia (2009)	The Reformulated OCS	Davis et al.'s (2002) OCS	10	Dependency Distraction	CFA	Reported	Reported (.61)

EFA aims to extract latent (common) factors that could reproduce the correlations among the observed variables based on the assumption that variation in a measured variable is due to variation in the common factor influencing that measured variable.

In contrast to PCA, EFA parses unique and common sources of variance and is thus thought to be a more appropriate technique for identifying latent factors (Fabrigar, Wegener, MacCallum and Strahan, 1999; Gorsuch, 1983; Widaman, 1993). Given these conceptual and mathematical differences, research has shown that principle components loadings tend to be overestimates of corresponding factor loadings (Widaman, 1993). Therefore, though PCA was used in the development of many PIU scales, EFA would have been the more appropriate tool given the objective of extracting latent factors, rather than data reduction.

Other than the choice between PCA and EFA, the determination of the number of factors to retain is probably the most crucial decision in either approach because retaining an incorrect number of factors can compromise the validity of the factor model and the resulting factor loading estimates (Brown, 2006). Having observed significant overfactoring in cognitive ability tests, Frazier and Youngstrom (2007) pointed out that one major cause for the factorially complex scales is a "heavy reliance on liberal statistical criteria for determining factor structure," such as Kaiser's criterion (i.e., eigen value greater than one), Cattell's scree test, and chi-square statistic resulting from maximum likelihood factor analysis. Though frequently used, these heuristics have been found to lead to significant overfactoring in the case of the Kaiser criterion and the chi-square statistic, or inconsistently recover the true number of factors in the case of scree test (e.g., Fabrigar et al., 1999; Frazier and Youngstrom, 2007). Thus, other more accurate criteria, such as Horn's parallel analysis (HPA; Horn, 1965) and Minimum Average Partial (MAP; Velicer, 1976) analysis, have been recommended in the psychometric literature as preferred criteria for factor extraction (Frazier and Youngstrom, 2007; Velicer, Eaton and Fava, 2000; Zwick and Velicer, 1986). Interested readers are referred to these studies for details about these two criteria.

However, as detailed later in this section, regardless of which decision rules are used in EFA/PCA for factor retention, both are exploratory or descriptive in nature, and neither can conclusively establish factorial validity. As Thatcher and Goolam (2005) acknowledged, validity is only "partially established" using exploratory factor analysis (p. 805). It is thus essential to use analytic techniques that are confirmatory in nature.

CFA

Confirmatory factor analysis was employed in the development of six PIU measures. CFA differs conceptually from EFA and PCA in that the number of factors is specified prior to the analysis (Frazier and Youngstrom, 2007). CFA has been recommended by many psychometricians (e.g., MacCallum, Roznowski and Necowitz, 1992) because it allows for alternative a priori models differing in factor structure and complexity be specified and evaluated to determine the model with the best fit, and consequently, the number of factors measured by the data (Frazier and Youngstrom, 2007). Such tests of alternative CFA models can be effectively used to assess factorial validity.

The following conclusions can be drawn from the above discussion:

1. Though PCA was frequently used in PIU scale development, EFA was the more appropriate tool given the objective of latent factor extraction, rather than data reduction.
2. Overfactoring is likely a threat to scales developed using EFA/PCA along with conventional decision heuristics for factor retention.
3. EFA and PCA are exploratory or descriptive in nature and are not effective tools to comprehensively establish instrument validity.
4. CFA is a useful technique because it can evaluate alternative a priori models to identify the factor structure with the best fit.

Implications for Factorial Validity of the PIU Scales

Factorial validity typically requires evidence for convergent validity/ unidimensionality, and discriminant validity. Convergent validity requires that the measurement items that should be related are indeed related, and unidimensionality further requires that one single latent variable underlie each scale. Both can be assessed with an exploratory technique like EFA, but can be more conclusively established with CFA.

Discriminant validity requires that the factors within a multidimensional measure must be unique from one another. In the context of EFA/PCA, weak discriminant validity is often a result of overfactoring. For example, when measurement items that underlie the same latent factor, Z, are treated as tapping separate factors, Z_1 and Z_2, the domains of Z_1 and Z_2 will have considerable overlap, leading to high inter-factor correlation and low discriminant validity between the two. However, inter-factor correlations may not always be high enough to threaten discriminant validity as gauged by prevailing statistical guidelines. In other words, only more severe cases of overfactoring threaten discriminant validity. (However, low discriminant validity is not uniquely related to EFA/PCA studies; one could end up with overlapping factors in a CFA study if not all appropriate tests are performed.)

If the use of conventional decision heuristics in exploratory techniques has led to significant overfactoring in cognitive ability tests (Frazier and Youngstrom, 2007), did the same heuristics lead to overfactored PIU scales that were also developed with EFA/PCA? Without the original datasets used in these studies, it was not possible to reanalyze the data using alternative factor retention criteria to answer this question conclusively. However, many PIU scales have reported relevant results that can be further examined to shed some light on this issue.

There are two prevailing methods to assess discriminant validity. A straight-forward way, as referenced above, is to examine the levels of inter-factor correlations. MacKenzie, Podsakoff and Jarvis (2005) noted that discriminant validity becomes problematic as factor correlations approach .71 (thus 50% of variance is shared). The other approach is to test a pair of CFA models, one with the two latent factors allowed to freely covary, and the other with their covariance constrained to one. If the unconstrained model represents significantly better fit than the constrained model, then there exists evidence for discriminant validity between the two latent factors. Thus, without the original dataset, this method requires the use of the inter-item correlation matrix.

With these discussions of factorial validity in mind, we next examine the existing PIU scales.

Unidimensional Measures

Three unidimensional PIU measures are found in Table 1: the Internet Addiction Test (IAT, Young, 1998), the Internet Addiction Scale (Nichols and Nicki, 2004), and the Compulsive Internet Use Scale (CIUS, Meerkerk et al., 2009). We focus our discussion on convergent validity/unidimensionality since discriminant validity is more relevant to multidimensional scales.

Young (1998) did not report the use of factor analysis for the 20-item IAT, though subsequent work by Chang and Law (2008) provides evidence for its convergent validity/unidimensionality, which is reviewed in a later section. Nichols and Nicki's (2004) 31-item Internet Addiction Scale was developed with PCA, which can provide preliminary evidence for its convergent validity and unidimensionality.

Meerkerk et al. (2009) developed the 14-item CIUS with CFA and demonstrated its convergent validity/unidimensionality as well as factorial invariance over time and different respondent groups.

Multidimensional Measures

Because convergent validity is frequently reported or can be inferred, and is oftentimes less of a concern, the focus of this discussion will be on their discriminant validity of the ten multidimensional scales.

IAST and PIUS

As summarized in Table 1, no inter-item or inter-factor correlation matrix was reported for the five-factor IAST (Lin and Tsai, 2002) and the three-factor PIUS (Ceyhan et al., 2007), both developed with PCA using conventional decision rules. Though overfactoring and discriminant validity can be an issue for both, a reanalysis of the original data with more accurate factor extraction criteria, or future replication studies would be necessary to find conclusive evidence.

GPIUS, PIUQ (Thatcher and Goolam, 2005) and PIUQ (Demetrovics et al., 2008)

Though moderate levels of inter-factor correlations were reported for all three scales, the possibility of overfactoring cannot be ruled out, particularly the seven-factor GPIUS (Caplan, 2002), since all of them were developed using EFA/PCA along with conventional decision rules. Reanalyses of the original data with more accurate factor extraction criteria, or future replication work using confirmatory techniques is needed for further examination.

The Revised IAT

Using PCA along with Kasier's criterion and the scree plot, Chang and Law (2008) extracted three principle components from Young's (1998) single-factor Internet Addiction Test. A subsequent CFA test of the three-factor model found its overall fit to be satisfactory; chi-square difference tests of CFA models also provided some support for discriminant validity (i.e., $\Delta\chi^2$

values of 47.05, 4.95, and 8.47). However, the high inter-factor correlations (i.e., .83, .88, and .88) suggest considerable overlaps amongst the three principle components extracted (as much as 77.44% of the variance), calling into question the adequacy of its discriminant validity based on MacKenzie et al.'s (2005) criterion.

This example illustrates how exploratory techniques, when used in conjunction with the conventional factor retention heuristics, can lead to overfactoring and weak discriminant validity. What appear to be conceptually distinct factors may not be empirically distinguishable. One may conclude that the IAT is indeed a unidimensional measure.

Internet Use and Addiction Survey

The Internet Use and Addiction survey (Pratarelli and Browne, 2002) was developed using a combination of EFA and CFA techniques. The fit of the CFA model does not meet the recommended thresholds ($\chi^2/df = 5.50 > 3.0$, Hair et al., 2006 and $GFI = .76 < .90$, Hu and Bentler, 1995). Many items with low factor loadings, particularly those in the .2-.5 range, could have been dropped to improve model fit.

Chinese Internet Addiction Inventory

Development of the Chinese Internet Addiction Inventory (Huang et al., 2007) was also based on a combination of EFA and CFA techniques. The scale generally demonstrates good psychometric properties, and its overall model fit ($\chi^2/df = 3.33$) can be further improved to meet the threshold of 3.0 (Hair et al., 2006) after eliminating items with low factor loadings.

Online Cognition Scale (OCS)

Though CFA results of the four-factor OCS suggest satisfactory overall model fit (Davis et al., 2002), discriminant validity of the scale was not explicitly tested. The inter-factor correlation matrix reported in the study reveals that the first three factors (i.e., loneliness/depression, diminished impulse control, and social comfort) have correlations ranging from .70 to .76, which can potentially be a cause for concern since discriminant validity becomes problematic as factor correlations approach .71 (MacKenzie et al., 2005). This led to a further examination and reformulation of the OCS by Jia and Jia (2009), to be reviewed next.

The Reformulated OCS

Jia and Jia (2009) found the overall fit of the four-factor OCS to be less than satisfactory with data from a sample of college students ($\chi^2/d.f.$ = 3.98, *RMSEA* = 0.106, *GFI* = 0.67) with high correlations among the first three factors (over .9), which calls into question the adequacy of its discriminant validity (MacKenzie et al., 2005). Jia and Jia (2009) pointed out that since these three factors manifest the user's dependency on Internet use (which is distinct from the fourth factor, *distraction*, which refers to the user's avoidance of responsibilities through Internet use), it can be argued that they tap the same latent construct, which can be labeled *dependency*. The OCS was thus reformulated into a two-factor model, which demonstrated satisfactory fit (χ^2/df = 2.36, *RMSEA* = .07, *CFI* = .97, *NFI* = .95, *GFI* = .94, *AGFI* = .91) as well as the necessary convergent validity/unidimensionality, discriminant validity and nomological validity. The stability of the two-factor reformulation was also shown with data from a sample of working adults.

In sum, though limited reporting of results for some of these measures prevented an in-depth examination for each existing PIU scale, evidence related to overfactoring and/or weak discriminant validity was found in certain scales (e.g., The Revised IAT, the four-factor OCS). Though a possible benefit of a comprehensive measure is its ability to produce unique subtest profile patterns for different populations, which could inform intervention approaches, an instrument consisting of fewer factors can be similarly effective but much more efficient, if the researcher is not concerned about profile analysis (Nelson et al., 2007). However, regardless of whether a more or less comprehensive measure is preferred in a specific setting, instrument developers must not compromise on the psychometric properties of the measure being developed. Practices contrary to this principle can undermine the purpose of scientific measurement.

Based on this review, we recommend the single-factor, 14-item CIUS (Meerkerk et al., 2009) and the two-factor, 10-item Reformulated OCS (Jia and Jia, 2009) for use in future research. They both exihibit satisfactory psychometric properties, parsimony and factorial invariance across respondent groups. Though the other scales have their own advantages, further testing and refinement may be necessary.

Definitional Issues

Prior authors (e.g., Shaffer and Freed, 2005; Surratt, 2006) have examined a number of conceptual issues and key assumptions in the PIU and the broader addiction literature. In this section, we focus on certain definitional issues that have not received much attention before. We begin by a discussion of what a construct definition is and is not.

A construct definition refers to a statement specifying the main properties of the construct; it should not be a logical statement of a relationship (Melcher, 2006). When a construct is defined in terms of a relationship, both the property of the construct and its assumed consequences are specified, making it impossible to separately identify and measure the independent and dependent variables (Melcher, 2006). Commenting on definitional issues in addiction research in general, Shaffer and Freed (2005) similarly point out that "the benchmark must be independent of the disorder being judged. There must be independent validation…"

The definitional issues in the PIU literature are not only a lack of a consensus definition, but also the prevalence of "relationship definitions" (Melcher, 2006). For example, PIU has been defined as behaviors and cognitions associated with Internet use that result in negative personal and professional consequences for the user (Davis, 2001), or as the "use of the Internet that creates psychological, social, school, and/or work difficulties on a person's life" (Beard and Wolf, 2001). These two definitions are quite representative of the others in the literature in the sense that the phenomenon is defined in terms of its consequences. (This problem is clearly also present at the measurement level as many PIU factors summarized in Table 1 are related to consequences.) To become a viable scientific construct, the construct definition must be conceptually independent from its consequences in non-tautological terms so researchers and clinicians can identify the condition without knowing its consequences (Shaffer and Freed, 2005).

As discussed in the introduction, achieving a rigorous, consensus definition is a critical step before the true factor structure of PIU can be discovered. Since this is an nascent area of research, achieving a unified view requires more cumulative work, which is beyond what can be achieved here. Though we refrain from proposing a new PIU definition, we note that progress is being made in related areas that can inform our effort. For example, Shaffer and Freed (2005) theorized that for pathological gambling to become a legitimate primary disorder, it needs to be viewed as overwhelming and uncontrollable impulses, compromised bio-behavioral regulatory mechanisms, or both.

CONCLUSION

This chapter reviewed thirteen PIU measurement instruments with varying factorial structures. After examining the different factorial analytic techniques used and their implications for factorial validity, we recommended more use of CFA in future PIU instrument development since it allows for testing of alternative a priori models and more conclusive assessment of factorial validility. Where an exploratory technique is necessary, EFA will be more appropriate than PCA for the purpose of extracting latent factors, and more accurate factor retention criteria (e.g., MAP, HPA) should be adopted because conventional rules are known to lead to overfactoring (Frazier and Youngstrom, 2007). We hope that these discussions will heighten future researchers' awareness of these issues.

In view of these methodological considerations, the PIU measures were examined for their factorial validity. Two measures developed with CFA, i.e., the unidimensional, 14-item CIUS (Meerkerk et al., 2009) and the two-factor, 10-item Reformulated OCS (Jia and Jia, 2009) have been recommended for future empirical research because of their sound psychometric properties.

Unifying our data analytic approaches is of vital importance in this area of research. Since instrument validation is a process driven by both theory and empirical data, the use of rigorous factor analytic techniques will inform our endeavor toward a consensus view of the PIU phenomenon and contribute to a cumulative tradition in this literature.

Finally, we discussed a pervasive definitional issue in PIU research – the lack of definitional independence. PIU is frequently defined in relation to, rather than independent of, its consequences. Such "relationship definitions" are conceptually problematic and can lead to tautologies in empirical research.

We hope that our discussions on the methodological and definitional issues in PIU construct development are useful for future research in this area.

ACKNOWLEDGMENTS

Portions of this chapter have previously appeared in Jia and Jia (2009).

References

Beard, K.W., and Wolf, E.M. (2001). Modification in the proposed diagnosis criteria for Internet addiction. *CyberPsychology and Behavior, 4*, 377-383.

Brenner, V. (1997). Psychology of computer use: XLVII. Parameters of Internet use, abuse and addiction: The first 90 days of the Internet usage survey. *Psychological Reports, 80*, 879-882.

Brown, T.A. (2006). *Confirmatory Factor Analysis for Applied Research*. Guilford Press, p.23.

Caplan, S.E. (2002). Problematic Internet use and psychosocial well-being: Development of a theory-based cognitive-behavioral measurement instrument. *Computers in Human Behavior, 18*(5), 553–575.

Ceyhan, E., Ceyhan, A.A., and Gürcan, A. (2007). The validity and reliability of the Problematic Internet Usage Scale. *Educational Science: Theory and Practice, 7*(1), 411-416.

Chang, M.K., and Law, S.P.M. (2008). Factor structure for Young's Internet Addiction Test: A confirmatory study. *Computers in Human Behavior, 24*, 2597-2619.

Chou, C. (2001). Internet heavy use and addiction among Taiwanese college students: An online interview study. *CyberPsychology and Behavior, 4*, 573-585.

Chou, C., Condron, L., and Belland, J.C. (2005). A review of the review on Internet addiction. *Educational Psychology Review, 17*, 363-368.

Davis, R.A. (2001). A cognitive-behavioral model of pathological Internet use. *Computers in Human Behavior, 17*, 187-195.

Davis, R.A., Flett, G.L., and Besser, A. (2002). Validation of a new scale for measuring problematic Internet use: Implications for pre-employment screening. *CyberPsychology and Behavior, 5*, 331-345.

Demetrovics, Z., Szeredi, B. and Rózsa, S. (2008). The three-factor model of Internet addiction: The development of the Problematic Internet Use Questionnaire. *Behavior Research Methods, 40* (2), 563-574.

Fabrigar, L.R., Wegener, D.T., MacCallum, R.C., and Strahan, E.J. (1999). Evaluating the use of exploratory factor analysis in psychological research. *Psychological Methods 4*(3), 272–299.

Frazier, T.W. and Youngstrom, E.A. (2007). Historical increase in the number of factors measured by commercial tests of cognitive ability: Are we overfactoring? *Intelligence, 35*, 169-182.

Gorsuch, R.L. (1983). *Factor analysis*. 2nd ed. Hillsdale, NJ: Erlbaum.

Hair, J.F., Black, W.C., Babin, B.J. Anderson, R.E., and Tatham, R.L. (2006). *Multivariate Data Analysis*, Upper Saddle River, NJ: Prentice-Hall.

Horn, J.L. (1965). A rationale and test for the number of factors in factor analysis. *Psychometrika, 30*, 179−185.

Hu, L. and Bentler, P.M. (1995). Evaluating model fit. In R.H. Hoyle (ed.), *Structural Equation Modeling*, Thousand Oaks, CA: Sage, 76–99.

Huang, Z., Wang, M., Qian, M., Zhong, J. and Tao, R. (2007). Chinese Internet Addiction Inventory: Developing a Measure of Problematic Internet Use for Chinese College Students. *CyberPsychology and Behavior, 10*(6), 805-811.

Jia, R. and Jia, H.H. (2009). Factorial validity of problematic Internet use scales. *Computers in Human Behavior, 25*, 1335-1342.

Kraut, R., Patterson, M., Lundmark, V., Kiesler, S., Mukopadhyay, T., and Scherlis, W. (1998). Internet paradox: A social technology that reduces social involvement and psychological well-being? *American Psychologist, 53*, 1017-1031.

Lin, S.S.J., and Tsai, C.C. (1999). Internet addiction among high schoolers in Taiwan. *Presented at the Annual Meeting of the American Psychological Association*, Boston, MA.

Lin, S.S.J., and Tsai, C.C. (2002). Sensation seeking and internet dependence of Taiwanese high school adolescents. *Computers in Human Behavior, 18*(4), 411–426.

MacCallum, R., Roznowski, M., and Necowitz, L.B. (1992). Model modifications in covariance structure analysis: The problem of capitalization on chance. *Psychological Bulletin, 111*(3), 490−504.

MacKenzie, S.B., Podsakoff, P.M., and Jarvis, C.B. (2005). The problem of measurement model misspecification in behavioral and organizational research and some recommended solutions. *Journal of Applied Psychology, 90*, 710-730.

Meerkerk, G.-J., Van Den Eijnden, R.J.J.M., Vermulst, A.A. and Garretsen, H.F.L. (2009). The Compulsive Internet Use Scale (CIUS): Some Psychometric Properties. *CyberPsychology and Behavior, 12*(1), 1-6.

Melcher, A. (2006). Theory Development Standards, unpublished notes, Southern Illinois University, Carbondale, IL.

Nalwa, K., and Anand, A.P. (2003). Internet addiction in students: A cause of concern. *CyberPsychology and Behavior, 6*, 653-656.

Nelson, J.M., Canivez, G.L., Lindstrom, W.L., and Hatt, C.V. (2007). Higher-order exploratory factor analysis of the Reynolds Intellectual Assessment Scales with a referred sample. *Journal of School Psychology, 45*, 439-456.

Nichols, L.A. and Nicki, R. (2004). Development of a Psychometrically Sound Internet Addiction Scale: A Preliminary Step. *Psychology of Addictive Behaviors*, *18*(4), 381–384.

Pratarelli, M.E. and Browne, B.L. (2002). Confirmatory Factor Analysis of Internet Use and Addiction. *CyberPsychology and Behavior*, *5*(1), 53-64.

Scherer, K. (1997). College life on-line: healthy and unhealthy Internet use. *Journal of College Student Development, 38*, 655–664.

Shaffer, H.J. (1997) The Most Important Unresolved Issue in the Addictions: Conceptual Chaos. *Substance Use and Misuse*, *32*(11), 1573-1580.

Shaffer, H.J. and Freed, C.R. (2005). Assessment of Gambling-related Disorders. In D.M. Donovan and G.A. Marlatt (eds.), *Assessment of Addictive Behaviors*, (2nd ed.), NY, Guilford Press, 334-391.

Shotton, M.A. (1989). *Computer Addiction? A Study of Computer Dependency*. Bristol, PA: Taylor and Francis.

Surratt, C.G. (2006). *The Psychology of Netaholics*. NY: Nova Science Publishers.

Thatcher, A., and Goolam, S. (2005). Development and psychometric properties of the Problematic Internet Use Questionnaire. *South African Journal of Psychology*, *35*(4), 793–809.

Tobacyk, J.J. (1995). Final thoughts on issues in the measurement of paranormal beliefs. *Journal of Parapsychology*, *59*, 141-145.

Treuer, T., Fabian, Z., and Furedi, J. (2001). Internet addiction associated with features of impulse control disorder: Is it a real psychiatric disorder? *Journal of Affective Disorders, 66*, 283.

Velicer, W.F. (1976). Determining the number of components from the matrix of partial correlations. *Psychometrika*, *41*(3), 321−327.

Velicer, W.F., Eaton, C.A., and Fava, J.L. (2000). Construct explication through factor or component analysis: A review and evaluation of alternative procedures for determining the number of factors or components. In R.D. Goffin and E. Helmes (eds.), *Problems and solutions in human assessment: Honoring Douglas N. Jackson at Seventy* (pp. 41−71).

Whang, L.S., Lee, S., and Chang, G. (2003). Internet over-users' psychological profiles: A behavior sampling analysis on Internet addiction. *CyberPsychology and Behavior, 6*, 143-150.

Widaman, K.F. (1993). Common factor analysis versus principal component analysis: Differential bias in representing model parameters? *Multivariate Behavioral Research, 28*, 263-311.

Widyanto, L., and McMurran, M. (2004). The psychometric properties of the Internet Addiction Test. *CyberPsychology and Behavior, 7*, 443-450.

Young, K.S. (1996). Psychology of computer use: XL. Addictive use of the Internet: A case that breaks the stereotype. *Psychological Reports, 79*, 899–902.

Young, K.S. (1998). *Caught in the Net: How to Recognize the Signs of Internet Addiction and a Winning Strategy for Recovery.* NY: John Wiley

Zwick, W.R., and Velicer, W.F. (1986). Comparison of five rules for determining the number of components to retain. *Psychological Bulletin, 99*(3), 432–442.

In: Internet Addiction
Editor: Hannah O. Price
ISBN 978-1-61122-058-2

Chapter 3

ON-LINE PATHOLOGICAL GAMBLING: A NEW CLINICAL EXPRESSION OF INTERNET ADDICTION

***Pauline Gorse*[1,1] *and Michel Lejoyeux*[2,2]**
[1]Department of Psychiatry. Hospital Maison Blanche. Paris. France
[2]Department of Psychiatry. Hospital Bichat-Claude Bernard. AP-HP Paris, France and Hospital Maison Blanche

INTRODUCTION

On-line pathologiocal gambling corresponds to the addictive use of money games on the Internet. It represents a new form of Internet addiction. There is no consensual definition for on-line pathological gambling but pathological gambling in "real life" has one. American Psychiatric Association considers pathological gambling disorder as an Impulse control disorder (American Psychiatric Association, 1994). This behavior is a compulsive and uncontrolled behavior that aims to meet a desire and produces pleasure. The behavior is continued despite the fact that leads to difficulties, and it penetrates deeply into the social life of the patient. On-line pathological gambling thus

---

[1]paulinegorse@hotmail.com.
[2] Corresponding Author : Michel Lejoyeux. Department of Psychiatry. AP- HP, Hospital Bichat Claude Bernard. 75877 Paris Cedex 18. France. Phone : 33 1 40 25 82 62. Fax : 33 1 40 25 67 80. E-mail : michel.lejoyeux@bch.aphp.fr.

represents a modern and frequent form of pathological gambling. Online pathological gambling is a new form of addiction. The past decade has witnessed an increased expansion in the types of available gambling activities and their accessibility. Participation in Internet gambling is growing to. For many gamblers, Internet gambling may be an attractive new activity.

DEFINITIONS

Internet addiction is characterized by excessive or poorly controlled preoccupations, urges or behaviors regarding computer use and Internet access that lead to impairement or distress. There is no diagnosis criteria of the Internet addiction, although it has been proposed for inclusion in the next version of the Diagnostic and Statistical Manual of Mental Disorder (DSM). The Internet addiction is divided into subtypes by activity, such as excessive viewing of pornography, inappropriate involvement in online social networking sites or blogging, Internet shopping addiction, and excessive gaming and gambling.

Problem gambling behavior occurs when individuals gamble in a manner that exceeds their means, for example spending more time or money than they can afford, gambling which causes significant distress and distruption to their lives, such as neglect of other important commitments including relationships and employment. The impact of problem gambling extends beyond each individual resulting in serious personal and societal problems including financial, legal, employment, medical and psychological difficulties. Problem gambling is a significant cause of family distrubances including arguments, relationship breakdown, neglect of children, domestic violence and the development of gambling problems amongst children of problem gamblers [1,2]. Financial hardship (via debts and asset losses) may lead to legal consequences, such as bankrupcy, loans, or criminal acts to gain money [3]. Problem gambling is also associated with health consequences including stomach problems, hypertension, heart disease, insomnia and psychosomatic symptoms [1,2]. Pathological gamblers are highly likely to exhibit other pychiatric problems at the same time including anxiety and depressive disorders, substance use disorders (found in up to 50% of problem gamblers), suicidal ideation (experienced by between 48% and 70% of pathological gamblers) and suicide attemps (13-20%)[1,4,5].

EPIDEMIOLOGY

The Internet is becoming a basic feature of global civilization. Informative, convenient, and entertaining, the Internet has changed the ways people work and spend their leisure time. As of June 2007, 1.133 billion people used the Internet according to the Internet World Stats. Uncontrolled Internet use may have negative impacts on social, occupational, academic, marital and interpersonal adjustement. The international prevalence rates for Internet addiction range from 1.5% to 8.2% [6].

The public and commercial use of the Internet introduced the possibility of online gambling. Rapid expansion followed with increases in the number of online gambling sites, types of games available. In january 2008, there were 2132 Internet gambling web sites owned by 477 companies. Revenues of these web sites similary increased from approximately US$2.2 billion in 2000 to US$15.2 billion in 2006 [7,8].

Prevalence of online gambling in the general population appears to be relatively low, but increasing. International prevalence assessments indicate that 1.2-8.1% of the population gamble online [9]. There is actually no exact data on the proportion of online patholgical gamblers but the prevalence of problem gambling seems to be higher amongst samples of Internet gamblers than in land-based gamblers. A study from the United Kingdom Gambling Comission, the "British Gambling Prevalence Survey 2007", found that approximately 0.6% of the adult population had problem gambling issues; while among an online sample of 1920 Internet gamblers a substantial proportion were classifed as moderate (22.6%) or severe (20.1%) problem gamblers [10]. Similar levels of problem gambling have been found amongst university students who gamble online [11,12].

PHENOMENOLOGY

In addition to characteristics of pathological gambling (loss of control, social and familial negative consequences...), online pathological gamblers present the core components of addiction which are salience, mood modification, tolerance, withdrawal symptoms, conflict and relapse [14]. For an online pathological gambler, online gambling is the most important thing in his life; he uses gambling as a way of consistent modifying his mood, a medium to escape from negative affects; he builds up tolerance to gambling over time. He suffers from withdrawal effects such as feelings of intense moodiness, anxiety, depression, and irritability. Lastly, he is exposed to conflicts in his life as a result of playing online games excessively. These conflicts lead him to loose his family and his job because he just cannot stop playing; and he experiences relapse as he cannot go more than a few days without an irresistible urge to play again.

Two subtypes of on-line pathological gamblers have been described. In the first category, gamblers on-line were already pathological gamblers in "real life". For them, Internet is just a new medium for gambling. Like the "classical pathological gamblers", they are more likely to exhibit other psychiatric problems at the same time, including substance use disorders, mood and anxiety disorders, or personality disorder. They tend to experience have marital conflicts, employement problems. They generally appear to be a heterogeneous group but several factors including low socioeconomic status, lack of employement, low education levels and alcoohol abuse have been linked to greater rates of pathological gambling [15].

In a second group, can be found gamblers who discovered gambling through the Internet. Most of them are younger, in an adolescent problematic, have poor social support function. They also play video games on-line, have an excessive use of e-mail/text messaging. They generally use Internet to escape from the reality. Gambling is a compensatory channel for unsatisfying needs or motivations in their life. The anonymity of Internet gives to subjects with low self-confidence the chance to create a virtual life for themselves on the Internet [16].

Internet gambling can take many forms.

The online poker sites propose online poker tables which commonly offer Texas hold'em,Omaha, Seven-card stud and ring game structures. Players play against each other rather than the "house", with the card room making its money through "rake" and through tournement fees. Internet poker is of particular interest because of the curent popularity of poker. There are also a large number of online casinos in which people can play casino games such as roulette, blackjack, pachinko, baccarat and many others. These games are played against the "house" . Bookmakers, spread betting firms and betting exchanges offer a variety of ways to wager over the Internet on the results of sporting events, the most popular being fixed-odds gambling (bets made on the outcomes of sporting events or games) as opposed to live-action betting (bets made on real time propositions about outcomes within a sporting event). There are also a number of online bingo rooms offering games on the Internet.

When compared to non-Internet gamblers, Internet gamblers were more likely to be male, relatively young adults, single, well educated, and in professional/managerial employement [13]. Women represent only 5,5% of the research cohort. It is interesting to note that the patterns of Internet poker play evidenced by women in their sample were very similar to that of the men. The only signification difference was that women played for a shorter duration of time between their first and last sessions.

PSYCHOPATHOLOGY

Little is know about on-line pathological gambling psychopathological mecanisms, psychiatric comorbidities or personnality disorders. A study on the online poker gambling in university students investigated some of the predicting factors of problem gambling [17]. It shows that problem on-line players are more likely to swap genders when playing online. When you play online you have a character representation of you in the virtual world with a pseudo you have to choose. In the virtual world, you can be some one else.

Problem on-line players are undisciplined and spend over their allocated budget. This predicting factor is true for all forms of problem gambling. If players start playing with money over and above what they had originally budgeted for, the model of the study suggests that this will lead to higher rates of problem gambling, and a pooer financial outcome overall. It could be that players are chasing losses and are going “on tilt”. Going on tilt refers to a negative cognition and emotional state usually caused by losing, often unexpectedly, whereby play becomes considered even reckless.

They also played more frequently for longer periods of time. Some of them can play 14 hours a day. Length of playing refers to the permanence of the online virtual world, that is online and accessible 24 h a day, 7 days a week. This results suggests that longer hours of play predict problem gambling but not necessarly financial problem. There is a complex relationship between time spent playing, winning, and developing gambling problems. For instance, it could be that the nature of problem gambling is changing and producing a new breed of problem gambler. With online poker, it is possible to play thousands of hands per week with few money in games and lots of experience can be gained. Another new area is the possibility to play more than one table at one time (multi-tabling). Players say they could easily play eight tables or more and improve their hourly rate hugely without needing to play high stakes. They do it because the hope of winning increases amonts of money.

The logical question is why not go and play on a higher table? Because it is most likely that higher stake tables house better players that provide more risk. Smaller stake tables probably house less skilled players and are therefore less risk to the skilled player. Such a playing strategy was not possible until poker was introduced online. For example, a problem gambler can win a lot money, over than $1,000 per month, but he is facing lots of other problems related to time spent on the activity. It suggests that online poker may be producing a new type of problem gambler where the main negative consequence is loss of time rather than loss of money. This could have implications for problem gambling criteria; there may be more criteria relating to the consequences of time conflicts as opposed to financial consequences. Problem gambling was also best predicted by negative mood states after gambling online and negative mood states more generally [18].

SOCIOLOGICAL RISK FACTORS

Certain characteristics specific to Internet gambling present additional risks for developing gambling problems, such as [19]:

- the lack of control over participants and easier access for underage gambling
- the unlimited acess to gambling venues at home or work
- the fact that people can play with other people from the comfort of their home
- the number of types of gambling opportunities
- greater anonymity, this anonymity allowing users to engage in gambling without fear or stigma
- the solitary nature of play and immersive nature of the Internet
- the use of electronic payement
- the ability of players to gamble while under the influence of drugs or alcohol
- the harmful marketing practices

The suggestion that Internet gambling may encourage problematic behaviour is supported by findings that the prevalence of problem gambling is higher amongst samples of Internet gamblers than land-based gamblers. Furthermore, there is a social acceptability of this type of gambling especialy for online poker, which is promoted through television tournements and often involves celebrity players, together with availability, and the belief that this is predominantly a game of skill that can be mastered.

Concomitant with the apparition of Internet gambling, there has been a significant increase in the advertising of differents games or gambling opprtunities [20,21]. Almost all youths report being exposed to advertising for Internet gambling. This gambling advertissements promote gambling as entertaining, exciting , enjoyable and easy opportunity to make money. Humour, bright and flashy colours, use of celebrities, provocative females and glamour are prominent features of commercial gambling ads. Gambling advertissements regularly portray gambling as a glamourous lifestyle, filled with excitement and promoting a sense of fantasy [22]. Previous marketing and advertising research have reliably shown that repeated advertising increases recall and sales [23,24,25]. An empirical study tried to have a better understanding of the impact of gambling advertising on youth gambling behavior. A questionnaire ascertaining adolescents'awareness of gambling advertissements and their impact upon their behavior was administered to 1147 youth between the ages of 12 and 19 from schools in Quebec and Ontario. The results show that rather than promoting the initiation of gambling for non-gamblers, these advertissements appear to serve the function of maintaining and reinforcing established gambling habits, beliefs and behaviors. The majority of adolescents are well aware of the advertisements promoting most forms of gambling. But advertissements that contain messages that gambling can lead to a happier lifestyle would almost certainly attract adolescents, especially those experiencing gambling-related problems. This observation is corroborated by the fact that adolescence is often perceived as a stressful period where escape and fantasy help relieve feelings of inadequacy. Participants who positively viewed gambling ads also tented to express a desire to gamble and were experiencing gambling-related problems. they frequently report gambling to escape and relieve boredom is of concern. Youth problem gamblers thus appear as vulnerable to gambling advertisements. Gambling providers and regulators should take into account the impact of gambling advertissements on youth and vulnerable individuals.

Some web sites use others questionable strategies in order to grab any interested potential player surfing the net. They use demo games. A demo game is a freely distributed demonstration of an upcoming or recently released Internet game. Demos are typically released by the game's publisher to help consumers get a feel of the game. A canadian study [26] assessed the payout rates of the demo trials for 117 sites, followed by a count of the payout rate differences between the demo and real money session. Payout rate is operationally defined as the amount of money won diveded by the amount of money wagered, multiplied by 100. The results show that 39% of sites provided a payout of over 100% after the first 100 trials of the demo phase; it is clear that no site could offer payout rates over 100%, if so, it would soon file for bankrupcy. These sites do not keep the same rates when gamblers play for real money. Some Internet operators use inflated payout rates and erroneous information during the "demo" period in order to attract individuals to their sites and that will trigger some potential players to try their luck with real money games. In addition, other sites used marketing strategies reinforcing false beliefs about the notion of chance and randomness. For example, they focused on good results obtained in the demo trials and incited the players to use their skills with real money. They sent electronic mails both during and after the experiment referred to erroneous beliefs, and the illusion of control such as " practice really does make perfect", "you are one of our smartest fun players", and " based on your playing skills". We know that players' erroneous thoughts are directly related to gambling persistence [27,28,29,30].

In recognition of the potential riks involved with Internet gambling, it is essential that responsible gambling strategies be enacted to protect players. Despite the lack of regulation, Internet gambling sites have a corporate responsability to protect their consumers from harm in the best possible way. The use of pop-up messages may be a solution for encouraging self-awareness to increase responsible gambling and reduce the incidence of problem gambling [31]. A pop-up message is a graphical user interface display area, usually a small window, that suddenly appears ("pops up") in the foreground of the visual interface. Pop-ups can be initiated by a single or double mouse click or rollover (sometimes called a mouseover), and also possibly by voice command or can simply be timed to occur. A pop-up window must be smaller than the background window or interface; otherwise, it's a replacement interface. The advantage of using pop-up signs include that they capture attention and increase comprehension of messages, causing only a minor disruption to play. The use of pop-up messages can also be combined with audio alerts, which may be more effective than pop-ups alone. The theorical support for the implementation of pop-up messages as a responsible gambling strategy has been demonstrated, but it is essential that any approach be empirically verified to determine its efficacy.

CONCLUSION

On-line gambling is a general term for gambling using the Internet. Individuals who gamble on-line are at risk of acting in a problematic manner and developing gambling problems causing significant distress and disruption in their lives. Online gambling addiction is an addictive behavior which is defined besides the characteristics of pathological gambling, by the six core compenents of addiction: salience, mood modification, tolerance, withdrawal symptoms, conflits and relapse.

Online gambling is raising concerns that easy access to, anonymity, harmful marketing practices and social approval of gambling is exposing more people to the risks of gambling, increase the number of people in the general population with gambling-related problems, and exacerbate the difficulties of those already affected by gambling. Epidemiological analyses of Internet gambling are necessary to determine the extent of public health threat.

Concomitant with this new form of gambling, there has been a significant increase in the advertising of different games and gambling opportunities. People should know about the dangers of Internet gambling, which may put them at risk of developing gambling problems. This is especially the case for young individuals as they are constantly offered direct links to gambling sites when they surfing on the Internet, or exposed to gambling advertising on television. The development of responsible codes of practice and guidelines should be established. Gambling providers and regulators should heed the warnings about the impact of gambling advertisements.

REFERENCES

[1] Delfabbro, P. (2008). *Australiasian Gaming Review* (3rd ed.). Adelaide: Independent Gambling Authority.

[2] Griffiths, M. (2004). Betting your life on it. *British Medical Journal*, 329,1055-1056.

[3] Ladouceur, R., Boisvert, J. M., Pepin, M., Loranger, M., and Dumont, M. (1994). Social cost of pathological gambling. *Journal of Gambling Studies*, 10 (4), 399-409.

[4] Griffiths, M. (2007). *Gambling addiction and its treatment within the NHS: A guid for healthcare professionals*. London: British Medical Association.

[5] Petry, N. (2005). *Pathological gambling: Etiologiy, comorbidity, and treatment.* Washington, DC: American Psychological Association.
[6] Petersen KU, Weymann N, Schelb Y, Thiel R, Thomasuis R. Pathological Internet use- epidemiology, diagnostics, co-occurring disorders and treatment (Article in German) Forschr Neurol Psychiatr 2009; 77(5):263-71.
[7] Christiansen Capital Advisors. (2005). *Egaming Data Report.*
[8] Christiansen Capital Advisors. (2007). Global Internet gambling revenues estimates and projections (2001-2010).
[9] Williams, R., and Wood, R. (2007). *Internet gambling: a comprehensive review and synthesis of the litterature.* Report prepared for the Ontario Problem Gambling Research Centre, Guelph, Ontario.
[10] Wood, R., and Williams, R., and Lawton, P. (2007). Why do Internet gamblers prefer online versus land-based venues: Some preliminary findings and implications. *Journal of gambling Issues,* 20.
[11] Ladd, G. and Petry, N. (2002). Disordered gambling among university-based medical and dental patients: A focus on Internet gambling. *Psychology of addictive behaviors*, 16, 76-79.
[12] Griffiths, M., and Barnes, A. (2007). Internet gambling: An online emiridale study among students gamblers. *International journal of mental health and addiction.*
[13] Griffiths M, Wardle H, Orford J, Sproston K, Erens B. Sociodemographic correlates of Internet gambling: findings from the 2007 british gambling prevalence survey. *Cyberpsychol Behav* 2009Apr;12(2):199-202.
[14] Griffiths, M. D. (2005). A "comonents" model of addiction within a biopsychosocial framework. *Journal of Substance Use*, 10, 191-197.
[15] John W. Welte, Grace M. Barnes, William F. Wieczorek, Marie-Cecile O. Tidwell, John C. Parker. Risk factors for pathological gambling. *Addictive Behaviors* 29 (2004) 323-335.
[16] Hsing Fang Tsai and al. The risk factors of Internet addiction- A survey of university freshmen. *Psychiatry Research* 167 (2009) 294-299.
[17] Mark Griffiths . Jonathan Parke . Richard Wood. Jane Rigbye. Online Poker gambling in university students: Further findings from onlie survey. *Mental health Addiction* (2010) 8:82-89.
[18] Matthews N, Farnsworth B, Griffiths MD. A pilot study of problem gambling among student online gamblers: mood states as predictors of problematic behavior. *Cyberpsychol Behav*. 2009 dec;12(6):741-5.

[19] Derevensky, J. (2008). Youth gambling problems: the hidden addiction. In Y. Kamine and O. G. Buckstein (Eds), Adolescent substance abuse: Psychiatric comorbidity and high risk behaviors. New York: Haworth

[20] Wood, R., and Williams, R. (2007). Problem gambling on the Internet: Implication for Internet gambling policy in North America. *New media and Society*, 9,520-542.

[21] Najavits, L. M., Grymala, L. D., and George, B. (2003). Can advertising incraese awareness of problem gambling ? A statewide survey of impact. *Psychology of addictivve behaviors*, 17,324-327.

[22] Derevensky, J. L., Gupta, R., Messerlian, C., Mansour, S. (2009). *The impact of gambling advertisements on child and adolescents behaviors: A qualitative analysis*. McGill University.

[23] Burke Najavits, L. M., Grymala, L. D., and George, B. (2003). Can advertising incraese, R. R., and Srull, T. K. (1989). Competitive interférence and consumer memory for advertising. *Journal of consumer research*, 15, 55-68.

[24] Noel, H. (2006). The spacing effect: enhancing memory for repeated marketing stimuli. *Journal of consumer psychology*, 16, 306-320.

[25] Stout, P. A., and Bruda, B. L. (1989). Zipped commercials: are they affective? *Journal of advertising,* 18, 23-32.

[26] Serge Sévigny, Martin Cloutier, Marie-France Pelletier, Robert Ladouceur (2004) Internet gambling : misleading payout rates during the « demo » period. *Computers in Human Behavior* 21 (2005) 153-15

[27] Blaszczynski, A. (2000). *Overcoming Compulsive Gambling*. London: Robinson.

[28] Ladouceur, R., Sylvain, C., Boutin, C., and Doucet, C.(2002). *Understanding and treating pathological gamblers*. London : Wiley.

[29] Ladouceur, R., 1 Walker, M. (1998). The cognitive approche to understanding and treating pathological gambling. In A. S. Bellack, 1 M. Hersen(Eds.), *Comprehensive clinical psychology* (pp.588-601). New York: Pergamon.

[30] Toneatto, T, Blitz-Miller, T., Calderwook, K., Dragonetti, R., and Tsanos, A. (1997). Cognitive distortions in heavy gambling . *Journal of Gambling Studies*, 13, 253-266.

[31] Sally Monaghan (2009). Responsible gambling strategies for Internet gambling: The theorical and empirical base of using pop-up messages to encourage self-awareness. *Computers in human behavior*. 25(2009) 202-207.

In: Internet Addiction
Editor: Hannah O. Price
ISBN 978-1-61122-058-2

Chapter 4

INTERACTIONS BETWEEN THE INTERNET AND ADOLESCENTS' SEXUAL DEVELOPMENT

N. Zdanowicz, A. Crochelet, D. Jacques, and C. Reynaert
Psychosomatic Unit, Cliniques de Mont-Godinne, Université Catholique de Louvain, B 5530 Yvoir, Belgium

ABSTRACT

Aim: to bring to light potential interactions between the use of the Internet, in particular for sexual purposes, and sexual issues during adolescence, whether these be general (psychosomatic, personality, communicational) or specific (sexual orientation, sexual identity, couple). Method: confronting our clinical experience with information found in MEDLINE, PSYCARTICLE, PSYCINFO literature. Results: if numerous studies have been conducted on the Internet's impact on certain aspects of young people's sexuality (misogyny, traumatism, transsexualities,...) none have systemised their approach in function of the psychosexual developmental issues. By rereading and reclassifying these studies concerning their area of impact, if we fear possible consequences on various issues, nothing can allow us today to establish that these are inevitably negative. The most obvious example is when we compare young people's sexuality between those that are looking for sexual partners via the Internet and those that do not, the only differences found are virtual. On the other hand, with regards to young people with an already pre-existing developmental problem, the Internet seems to act as a catalyst aggravating the specific problem. In conclusion: at this moment in time, and considering the small number of studies that have actually been conducted with extremely varying methodologies, nothing allows for the generalisation that the Internet has a negative impact on adolescents' and young adults' sexuality.

Keywords: Sexual development – adolescent – Internet

I. Introduction

There are numerous sexual issues during adolescence, it is during this time that the style of sexuality is determined, whether it be the choice of the sexual identity, the manner in which sexuality is experienced or yet still the sexual orientation. Since the 1990's, with the Internet boom, adults wonder about the effect of sexual contents on adolescents' sexuality. In a previous article [1] we reviewed the literature that exists on the possible disorders. Our objective this time is to try to investigate the links that exist between these disorders and the psychosexual development.

Investigating these links is complicated as 4 filters exist that deform observations:

1. Adolescence and its manifestations vary within one same society depending on the era (adolescence in the 60's is not the same as in the 80's nor is it the same as in the 2000's).
2. Sexuality in a society varies regarding the era. Thus, sexuality during the interwar period, the 60's or yet still after the outbreak of AIDS is not the same.
3. Sexuality in a society varies first of all with adolescents. They are the ones that influence the new manners of experiencing sexuality.
4. Adults imagine that adolescents' sexuality is more worrying than it really is. The most well known example is the statement that there are more and more teenage pregnancies in Western countries. Other misguided statements also exist: that the age of the first sexual experience has significantly decreased or that young people do not use protection against AIDS.

The example regarding the overestimation of teenage pregnancies is an interesting one as it was used to justify a clarification made by Unicef in 2001 [2]. In reality, the number of teenage pregnancies in the West has been decreasing constantly for practically the last 30 years, although it is true that the scores vary greatly between the Anglo-Saxon and Western European countries. In the Netherlands, the risk of teenage pregnancies is at $8.1/_{00}$ whereas in the United States it is at $9.3/_{00}$. In Belgium, in 1998, there were 14000 abortions in total that were done where "only" 1700 of them were for those under the age of 19. Less than 50% of these young people were using contraception. The important differences that exist between these different countries are, according to certain authors, due to the manner in which the adults try to "manage" young people's sexuality. The worst scores are found in the countries that want to prevent and to legislate against having sex before marriage (United States), the intermediate scores are found in England where the position is to try to delay as much as possible the age of first time sex, the best scores are obtained in Sweden and the Netherlands where the belief is that adolescent sexuality exists and that it is the risks that need to be prevented.

Similarly as with the rate of teenage pregnancies, the press regularly claims that the age of the first sexual encounter is more and more low. This statement is also false. The age of the first sexual encounter in 1990 is 17 years of age whereas in 1960 it is 20 years of age. In 30 years, the age only altered by 3 years, and since 1990 the age of the first sexual encounter has practically not changed [3, 4]. Under 17 years of age, there are only a minority of young people that have a sexual relationship. Though, it is true, that more than one out of two teenagers that has a premature sexuality (15 years old) has more than one partner.

With regards to AIDS, adults are terrified by young people's lack of knowledge and senseless risk-taking. This statement is also false. Since 1990, practically 100% of adolescents correctly identify the risk of transmission that exists between people. Though it is true that even if the percentage of young people that know that an asymptomatic person car infect another is high in 2002 [5], 20% of these teenagers continue to doubt that this risk really exists. In addition, if the condom is widely used by young people, the proportion of those that use one is significantly less so among teenagers that have had several partners. Among these, 2/10 expose themselves to a real risk, one that is even higher when alcohol or drugs are regularly consumed.

In order to study the links between the Internet and young people's sexuality, we have separated into two parts the description adolescence's sexual modifications: a) general modifications and b) specific modifications.

With regards to the general modifications, two levels of change can be distinguished on:

1. the psychosomatic unity's functioning,
2. the personality development and communicational capacities.

The specific modifications can also be subdivided into three levels of change on:

1. the body,
2. the sexual identity and sexual orientation,
3. the couple.

II. METHOD

Our article is principally based on our clinical practice with adolescents in a university hospital that has sexual health and adolescent consultations. Aside from this clinical experience, we have confronted our hypotheses with the bibliographical research done: on medline – psycinfo – psycarticles by using the following keywords: adolescence, sexuality, sexual orientation. We have also consulted reference books.

III. RESULTS

A. General Sexual Modifications

1. General Sexual Modifications: Psychosomatic

Out of the numerous health definitions that one can give, the most often given by adolescents is that health is above all the body's silence, the absence of pain. Because they don't feel pain they describe themselves as healthy [6]. Bearing this in mind, the rapid modifications of the adolescent's body's morphology (secondary sexuation) is the absolute opposite of silence, these body changes make "noise". They are suspected to be at the origin of the multiple somatic and hypochondriac complaints that explain the increase in pediatric consultations during adolescence. Indeed, if we count one consultation between the ages of 0 and 10, 9 additional consultations are counted between the ages of 10 and 18. The cause analysis of these 9 additional consultations reveals that they are without a somatic explanation [7]. The secondary sexual modifications are destabilising less so by their magnitude (for example a change in height) than by the speed at which these changes happen. If we have between 40 and 50 years to get used to our aging bodies, an adolescent only has a few years with his or her body's transformation from a child's body into an adult's body. Similarly to Alice in Lewis Carol's novel, the adolescent has to rapidly relearn how to adapt to his or her body and reintegrate a new body image. We can fear that if a young person has not yet experienced nor learnt about these transformations, being faced with pornographic images off the Internet could provoke a traumatism. Hayez [8] believes that this is the case for a minority of adolescents for whom these images can have a destabilising effect by confronting the young person to his or her body changes before these have been integrated. However, this risk seems to be relatively limited as, according to Kanuga and al [9], if 70% of young people between 15-17 years of age were confronted with pornographic websites involuntarily, 97% say that they are not traumatised. Nonetheless, in another study Mitchell KJ and al [10] with a younger sample of adolescents, found very high stress levels in 20 to 25 % of them.

2. General Sexual Modifications: Personality Development and Communicational Capacities

Physical sexuation is for the majority of adolescent crisis' theorists the driving force behind the psychological changes and, in particular, the relational changes that occur during adolescence. The most obvious example of change in the relational behaviour appears with the parent of the opposite sex due to the adolescent's body being sexualised. Physical proximity is now experienced with embarrassment and leads to progressive distancing. With these two changes, a "noisy" body and a transforming relational system, the body becomes a place of transition, with reference to Winnicott's meaning [11]. The transition is between the body and the behaviour of a child and the body and behaviour of an adult. This transitional body is a means of written, imaginary or real communication. Written by marks (piercing, tattoo,...) done by the adolescent, imaginary by his or her look and different styles of dressing tried out that are more or less sexualised, and finally real as the behaviour is no longer that of a child, nor is it completely that of a sexualised adult.

The Internet can interact by promoting oversexualised behaviours too early on. Indeed, one knows that the younger the models on these websites are the more the adolescent is at risk of identifying (him or herself) with him or her [12]. There is a risk that the sexual stimuli protective shield from childhood allows the images of these young models engaged in pornographic behaviours through. These premature behaviours may as a consequence not be identified as "abnormal" for that age group. On top of this they are normalised by the fact that they are accessible by all on the Internet. Though studies do show that this risk is limited: there is only a 6 month difference in age regarding a first real sexual experience between the young people that look for sexual partners on the Internet and those that do not [13]. Similarly, the number of real sexual experiences per year between these 2 sample groups is practically superimposable. Lastly, if the first sexual protective shield during childhood are the parents, adolescents are capable of finding others. Cooper [14] has highlighted the fact that Internet users protect their identity with numerous lies: on their age, their sex and their picture.

B. Specific Sexual Modifications

1. Specific Sexual Modifications: Bodily

The sexual bodily modifications are as much visual, emotional as they are somesthetic. Visual: the adolescent has now to take into account the effect that his or her sexualised body has on his or her relational system. The new image acquired can now act as a means of sexual seduction and take part in his or her first flings. If up until now relations with pairs have been relatively asexual the adolescent must at this point take into account the difference of sexes. But, before regarding others, the body's sexuation also intervenes in the adolescent's rapport with him or herself. The adolescent has to get used to his or her new sexualised image and endeavour to appreciate it, with its sexual attributes, in order to acquire a minimum of self-esteem.

Regarding the affective modifications that exist, other than the detachment from parents, there is also the construction of the first romantic relationship. This is built via a mirror image: the knowledge of the body and feelings transit from one to the other [15]. If this relationship establishes an identity rapport, it also allows the construction of alterity to be done through experimenting sexual differences whether these are physical or psychological.

Finally, on a somesthetic level, the adolescent experiments sensations that were up until then unknown: first periods or nocturnal ejaculations, autoerotic caresses that become heteroerotic, and lastly first sexual relations.

The body's sexuation and image is at this age a driving force in the construction of the identity and the difference between sexes. The dreaded impact of the Internet is a certain blending of differences, and in particular of sexual differences. The identity construction is undertaken in a relatively unisex mode with scarcely differentiated limits regarding others. These effects are obtainable notably through virtual communities such as MySpace and Facebook [16, 17]. The sexual identity is limited to a photograph and a number of friends that is disproportionate in comparison to real life. The number of friends per subscriber varies between 150 and 1000. With such a number of relationships to take care of it is obviously impossible to build a real friendship. Not only is the relationship submerged by the vast amount of other friends but also if the "friend" appears to be too different – disappointing – he or she can easily be excluded. Furthermore, to maintain a virtual network such as this can only be done at the cost of real friendships. Lastly, the amount of important private information that is put online and shared with such a large number of people can also lead to the dissolution of the frontier that exists between what is personal and public.

If these impacts can be feared, Manago [16] and al have however shown that:

- the differences of sex are accentuated by young people through a series of artifices such as the choice of colour for their Internet page (pink for girls, blue for boys) and the contents (pictures of sports cars for boys,…).
- body image remains important as is demonstrated by the computer improvements that have been made regarding personal photographs. The adolescents touch up their pictures, or even come to lie about their photo by using another one of someone else who is "better looking". This type of process can even add, on the contrary to the depreciation of the importance of image, to the overestimation of beauty. The risk is that if a person does not correspond with the standards of beauty they will have to incessantly compare themselves to profiles that are sexier than his or her own.
- this type of bonding community allows the youngster that has to change environment (for example leave his or her village to go to a university campus where he or she does not know anybody) to reduce his or her future isolation. The young person can makes contacts and establish ties with students that are already residing on the university campus. By doing this he or she reduces his or her risk of future isolation and, in turn, Internet dependency [18].

REFERENCES

[1] Salmon Y, Zdanowicz N. Net, sex and rock'n'roll ! The potentialities of a tool like the internet and its influences on a teenagers' sexuality. *Journal of Sexology*. 2006;54(2006):1158-360.
[2] Daguerre A., Nativel C. Record américain. *Le monde diplomatique*. 2003;12:12.
[3] Piette D., Favresse D., Houioux G., De Smet P. Huitième enquête sur les comportements de santé des jeunes scolarisés en Communauté française Bruxelles2006.
[4] Piette D., Prevost M., Boutsen M., de Smet P., Leveque A., Barette M. *Vers la Santé des jeunes en l'an* 2000? . Bruxelles: ULB; 1997.
[5] Piette D., Parent F., Coppieters Y., Favresse D., Bazelma,s C., Kohn L., De Smet P. La santé et le bien-être des jeunes d'âge scolaire. *Quoi de neuf depuis* 1994? Bruxelles2003.
[6] Zdanowicz N. La santé à l'adolescence: un processus d'internalisation lié à la dynamqiue familiale. Louvain La Neuve: *Faculté de Médecine*; 2001.
[7] Marcelli D., Braconnier A., editor. *Adolescence et psychopathologie*. Paris: Masson; 2008.
[8] Hayez JY. La confrontation des enfants et des adolescents à la pornographie. *archives pediatrics*. 2002;9:1183-8.
[9] Kanuga M., Rosenfeld W. Adolescent sexuality and the internet: The good, the bad and the URL. *Journal of Pediatric and Adolescent Gynecology*. 2004;17:117-24.
[10] Mitchell K., Finkelhor D., Wolack. J. Risk factors and impact of online sexual solicitation of youth. *JAMA*. 2001;2005:3011-4.
[11] Winnicott DW. Jeux et réalité. Paris: *Gallimard*; 1971.
[12] Zdanowicz N., Reynaert C. Medicine student's knowledge in sexology and their use of Internet. *Sexologies*. 2007;16:121-31.
[13] Cooper A., Sherer C., Mathy R. Overcoming Methodological Concerns in the Investigation of Online sexual Activities. *Cyberpsychology Behaviour*. 2001;4:437-47.
[14] Cooper A., Mcloughlin MI, Campbell K. Sexuality in Cyberspace, Update for the 21st century. *Cyberpsychology Behaviour*. 2000;3:521-36.
[15] Zdanowicz N. Les premières passions à l'adolescence. *Cahier de Psychologie Clinique*. 1993;1:87-98.

[16] ManagoA. M., Graham M.B., Greenfield' P.M., Salimkhan G. Self-presentation and gender on MySpace. *Journal of Applied Developmental Psychology*. 2008;29:446-58.

[17] Subrahmanyam K., Reich S., Waechter N., Espinoza G. Online and offline social networks: Use of social networking sites by emerging adults. *Journal of Applied Developmental Psychology*. 2008;29:420-33.

[18] Wirion M., Zdanowicz N., Pull C., Hidgen M. L'Internet est-il un outil de communication pathologique ou non ? . *Annales medico-psychologiques*. 2004;162:477-87.

[19] van Meerbeeck P. L'infamille Ou La Perversion Du Lien. Bruxelles: *De Boeck*; 2003.

[20] McFarlane M., Bull S., Rietmeijer C. Young adults on the Internet: risks behaviours for sexually transmitted diseases and HIV. *Journal of Adolescent Health*. 2002;31:11-6.

[21] CooperA. Sexuality and the Internet: Surfing into New Millenium. *Cyberpsychology Behaviour*. 1998;1:187-93.

In: Internet Addiction
Editor: Hannah O. Price

ISBN 978-1-61122-058-2

Chapter 5

AN INSPIRATION FROM INTERNET ADDICTION MAL-TREATMENT IN CHINA

C. H. Lau, Sian M. Griffiths and Jean H. Kim
School of Public Health and Primary Care,
The Chinese University of Hong Kong

ABSTRACT

Although psychology and psychiatry experts around the world continue to debate the nature and definition of internet addiction (IA), there have been widespread efforts to treat youths exhibiting pathological cyber use in China. It is estimated that more than 300 treatment centres have been established throughout China and that they have accumulated a gross income in excess of US$100 million since the mid-2000s. Non-evidence-based therapies, using unscientific and inhumane approaches are, however, pervasive such as the misuse of psychotropic medication, solitary confinement, excessive physical punishment, and involuntary electroconvulsive therapy. The rapid and uncontrolled expansion of IA treatment industry in China is attributable to the country's unique political and socio-economic environment, giving rise to the urgent need to standardize the definition of internet addiction for contemporary public health workers and to develop evidence-based treatments.

INTRODUCTION

The Peoples' Republic of China (PRC) has the highest absolute number of internet users in the world. In 2010, there were 384 million regular internet users, more than the total population of the United States.[1] Although the number of internet users in China has increased by 22-fold between the year 2000 and 2010, the internet penetration rate is still less than 30%. China's comparatively low penetration rate, as compared to developed countries in the West, thereby indicates that much of the growth in Internet use may be yet to come. Young people comprise the majority of the cyber population in China. Compared with the overall penetration rate of 28.7%, 54.5% of the people aged 25 or younger are internet users, accounting for 50.7% of total users.[2]

Originating in the United States, the idea that internet use could be addictive was raised in mid 1990s. By adopting the DSM-IV definition of pathological gambling, Kimberly Young proposed eight diagnostic criteria for internet addiction (IA) in 1996.[3] Ten years later, the question of whether IA should be included as a diagnosis in DSM-V remained a controversial topic among psychologists and psychiatrists.[4,5] The American Psychiatric Association decided not to include IA in the draft of DSM-V, but "will be considered as potential additions as research data accumulate".[6] Although there was lack of golden standard, numerous studies had shown that excessive internet use or IA was related to poor mental health (e.g. low self-esteem, depression, loneliness) and unhealthy life style (physical inactive, poor sleeping habit, skipping meals). Young people, particularly students, were considered as the most vulnerable risk group for IA.[7,8]

Concomitant with the burgeoning numbers of internet users, the numbers of pathological internet users in China will undoubtedly also increase rapidly. As shaped by China's unique socio-economic and political environment, internet addiction has different implications for the country. Nowhere has IA been a more popular and controversial topic than in China. IA is not only viewed as a psychological and social topic, but also a political and even commercial issue. This article will provide reflections on the current understanding of IA in China by discussing two recent cases of IA treatment.

Case One: Perfectly Successful Treatment

In 2006, a psychiatric hospital in Shandong Province started to admit patients who were thought to be addicted to the internet. In a patent application, they claimed that they had cured 300 internet addicts with a success rate of 100% with a Chinese herbal tea combined with psychological treatment.[9]. Yang Yongxin, head of the centre, was awarded the title of "Ten Outstanding Shandong Citizens of Minor Protection" in 2007 for his incredible achievement of rehabilitating 500 young people from web addictions.[10] In 2008, he appeared on the China Central Television (CCTV), the official television broadcast channel of China, helping him to ascend to the position of a premier IA specialist in China. Drawing the attention of the central government, Dr. Yang obtained a special subsidy for outstanding scientists from the state council until a full page expose published in the China Youth Daily (the official newspaper of the Communist Youth League) in 2009 uncovered medical malpractices. [11] Dr. Yang's centre was described by *Science* as "the most infamous" centre.[12] What happened to the "IA patients" in the psychiatric hospital?

In this centre, patients were called *Alliances*, for a reason of "destigmatization". New alliances had to hand over their mobile phone, mp3 player, and their internet passwords. A list of 86 rules which disallowed not only internet use, but also eating chocolate and locking door when using the toilet. Some parents stayed in the centre with their children and they formed a parent committee as part of the administrative system, monitoring all alliances and facilitating the treatment. [11-14]

After all, the centre's ultimate weapon was the DX-IIA, an electroconvulsive therapy (ECT) machine that had been banned by the country in 2000. Every new alliance to the centre was treated with ECT, until he or she confessed as "internet addicts" and was willing to stay. Although Yang described his ECT as "very painful but not harmful", survivors said that was a feeling of "stabbed by a thousand swords" and incontinence was common during the electric shock. Violating any rules would possibly lead to ECT. Alliances learnt that if they pretend to be so regretful and beg for ECT, they might be able to escape from it. [11-14]

Case Two: Deadly Summer Camp

Deng Senshan, a 16-year old boy in Guangxi Province, had just completed his junior secondary education. On a summer evening in 2009, Senshan's father, as many other Chinese parents, watched a programme introducing a "rescuing training camp" dedicated to young internet addicts. Frustrated because they could not stop their son's incessant net surfing, Senshan's parents decided to send their only child for some "hard experience". The parents arrived at the training camp with Senshan. Before handing over their son to the centre, they signed an agreement with the centre, in which the centre promised that they would not abuse the child or do harm to his physical health. The parents never imagined that their son would be dead within 13 hours, with an anatomical report stating that "death was due to respiratory and cardiovascular collapse due to acute respiratory distress syndrome, secondary to multiple soft tissue injury".[15,16]

Police cracked down on the centre and 122 trainees were released. Four "training officers" aged 19 to 23 were charged with intentional assault, whereas two were students of a normal university as summer employees. In court, it was revealed that all new trainees to the camp were confined for 24 hours, which they were not allowed to eat, drink, sleep, or crouch, but "stand upright, face the wall and have introspection". Senshan was beaten by the officers using rods and whips, with other trainees holding him on the ground, as he refused the confinement and was unable to complete a 10km run. Although he showed symptoms of shock at midnight, he was not sent to hospital until 3 A.M., when he was declared dead. In May 2010, two defendants were respectively sentenced for 5 and 10 years imprisonment and the other two with suspended sentence.[17,18]

Since mid-2000s, IA treatment centres have mushroomed all over China. It was estimated that more than 300 centres were established throughout the country, even though the Ministry of Health has never formally sanctioned IA treatment. The stories such as those of Yang and Deng were not rare instances. The use of ECT was also reported in Guangdong Province. [19]Cases of serious injury and death were repeatedly reported in military-style IA camps in different areas.[10]. Despite their advertised claims of very high success rate, the efficacy of such "IA therapies" is basically unknown. However, not surprisingly, there were obvious side effects. A victim of involuntary ECT had suffered from multiple atrial fibrillation after he fled from the centre. [20] Many of the children became hostile towards parents. Returning from an IA school, the first thing one 16-year old boy told his parents was that he would not study anymore or get married in the future, as he had devoted the rest of his life to make them suffer. Another boy, suffering from repeating nightmares of being sent to Yang's centre again, reported studying hard for university entrance because "staying at home was very dangerous".[19,13] A drug addiction treatment centre in Ningbo utilized medicine for drug abusers to treat internet addicts, leading to anhedonia and lethargy in the patients.

[21]The prevalence of unscientific and inhumane approaches to treat IA, however, was closely related to China's socio-economic and political environment. In the following, perspectives of different stakeholders will be examined, which will provide a full picture of the problem.

Perspective of the Chinese Communist Party and Government

> "Decadent culture and harmful information are spreading through the internet, corrupting the minds of our youths"
>
> --- Communist Party of China Central Committee and State Council, 2004

Ever since the Communist Party of China (CPC) gained sovereignty of mainland China in 1949, it has had firm control over the ideology of the country. As the internet has become a new platform of expression and information exchange, Chinese officials take a cautious view of it. The government has taken a hardline stance over the control of internet-based information, similar to that of other traditional media platforms. Operated by Ministry of Public Security, China has one of the most comprehensive internet censorship systems in the world, often known as "The Great Firewall". It aims to filter and monitor any sensitive activities in politics, religious, and pornography on the cyberspace. The censorship is imposed to all net users in the country, including foreign companies providing internet service in China. As a refusal to cooperate with the policy, Google, the world's leading search engine and GoDaddy, the world's leading domain name registrar have withdrawn from the China market in 2010. [22]

In addition to internet censorship in general, the Communist Party was particularly concerned about the effect of the internet on young people. In 2004, the Communist Party Central Committee and the State Council published a document for "*strengthening and improving the work on minor's mind*", which averred that although the internet worked as a new channel of study and entertainment, it also spread information that corrupted the mind.[23]. In response to this document, the responsible office in CPC had run a nationwide anti-IA program since 2005. The program promoted both basic research and intervention.[24] Although no concluding remark could be drawn from the programme, local governments had started to implement IA intervention in their own ways, which promoted the unregulated expansion of the IA treatment industry.[10]

In addition to specific efforts put on IA, “protecting minors” was also a common reason for the Chinese government to control the internet. Cyber cafes, where many young people use the internet, had became a major focal point of this movement. Following a fire which killed 25 people in a Beijing cyber café in 2002, the government has stopped issuing any new licenses for cyber-cafes, except for those operating as a chain across the country. Since 2002, minors have been prohibited from entering cyber cafes. For many years, while the annual centralized examination was approaching, some local governments closed all cyber cafes for a month in order to “maintain a good environment for studying”. [25]

In addition to cyber cafes, the government also tried to control computer use at home. In 2009, the Ministry of Industry and Information Technology published a content-control software called the Green Dam Youth Escort. The software, which was said to “avoid poisoning of our youth's minds by harmful information”, filtered political, religious, and pornographic content on the web. It also allowed parents to restrict time of internet use, monitor the usage log, and prohibit the use of instant messengers and online games. The Ministry required that since July 2009, all computers selling in the country shall pre-install GDYE. Due to pressure from internal and external businesses, this mandatory requirement was stopped before general implementation, but was still applicable to computers in schools, cyber cafes, and other public venues. [26]

Perspective of Medical and Behavioral Scientists

Due to the lack of golden standard definition of IA, medical and behavioral scientists around the world define and measure IA in different ways and comparison across different studies is difficult.[7,27] In China, the nature and definition of IA is also a hot topic among researchers; moreover, these researches face an even greater problem of inconsistent criteria.

Since IA was first proposed in the West, most IA studies in China are based on translated instruments. The 8-question Internet addiction Diagnostic Questionnaire by Young,[3] as the earliest measurement tool of IA, is still most commonly used in China due to its simplicity. Some researchers, however, extended the Young’s Diagnostic Questionnaire to 10 items whilst retaining the original cut-off point of 5, which would inevitably define more people as internet addicts. [28]The 20-item Internet Addiction Test (IAT), also developed by Young,[29] is widely adopted with different variations with different cut-off points. Attempts have also been made to compound different criterion, such as defining IA as Diagnostic Questionnaire score ≥ 5 and modified IAT ≥ 50.[30]

In addition to adopting measurements from the West, Chinese researchers also attempt to invent their own criteria for IA. The most popular one of these is the Chen's Internet Addiction Scale, which was developed in Chinese in Taiwan. The 26-item scale has a cut-off point of 64/104 for adolescents, and is validated by psychiatric interviews.[31] Bai and Fan in Mainland China reduced Chen's scale into 19-item (CIAS-R-19) based on a factor analysis among a group of university students in Beijing, and defined the 95th-percentile among the respondents (53/76) as the cut-off point.[32] The original and the abbreviated Chen's Scale are both commonly found in Chinese IA studies.

Despite the lack of consensus in the definition, much research is focused on studying IA among students, as encouraged by government policy. Hundreds of related study reports can be identified on databases of Chinese journals. Although the modifications to foreign criteria might be essential to addressing the cultural difference, the rationale of making such changes has been rarely documented. This not only hinders any meaningful comparison across studies, but also renders the validity of these studies doubtful.

In 2008, TAO Ren, who had been implementing drug therapy to net addicts in Beijing for years, announced the country's first diagnostic criteria of IA and submitted that to MOH for approval.[33] The full criteria were published later in *Addiction* in 2010. [34]TAO Hongkai, another famous IA expert using counseling as the primary strategy, criticized it as medicalization of a psychological problem for the sake of profit. A principal of an IA school in Jiangxi believed that the criteria should be set by the Communist Party of China. [35]Eventually, the Ministry of Health did not approve the proposal. In a consultation document published in 2009, the Ministry of Health announced that "The definition of IA remains unclear. It should not be used to assess the damage towards physical health and social functioning caused by improper use of the internet". [36]As of June 2010, China still does not officially recognize any diagnostic definition for IA.

Perspective of Chinese Parents

In addition to the above mentioned factors, the high demand of parents was probably the main driving force behind the burgeoning IA treatment industry in China. Parents, rather than the purported internet addicts, represent the actual customers of these treatment centres since they elect to send their children there and pay for the treatment. For a treatment centre like the one Deng Shensan was sent to, which used retired soldiers and students as training officers, the running cost for each trainee could be only 1000 Renminbi (US$146) per month, just a tiny fraction of 7000 Renminbi treatment fee paid by Shensan's parents. In 2009, the CCTV estimated that Yang's ECT centre had accumulated a gross income of 81M Renminbi (US$11.8M) and the whole industry was grossing more than a billion Yuen.[10,37]

The eagerness of Chinese parents to treat their internet-addicted children is closely related to the social and culture background of China's "one-child policy" that was launched in 1978. Although the primary objective of this national policy was to control the rapidly growing population, the secondary purpose was to increase the quality of the new generation. Chinese parents were forced to concentrate all their resources and expectations on their only child. China's exam-oriented education system cultivates only a small proportion of elite individuals, hence, academic success became a commonly held parental expectation of their child. Excessive internet use, which inevitably is in conflict with high academic success, was therefore seen as a major enemy of the parents.[38,39]

The mass media has also played an important role in creating parental prejudice of towards the youth internet use. Consistent with the official standpoint, IA among young people was often depicted by the media as a pressing problem of the country, which seriously affected their academic performance and invariably led to deviant and even illegal behaviors. Centres that showed remarkable achievement in the area of IA rehabilitation, such as Yang Yongxin's centre, were lauded by official media. Advertisements and advertorials of IA schools, such those seen by Deng Shensan's father, were highly visible in major newspapers and television channels. Exaggerated claims were commonplace and propaganda-type messages were often employed in order to convince parents that they were the saviors of their internet-addicted children.

Attempts to Control

Following the scandals of application of violent and inhumane measures in IA treatment, the Ministry of Health attempted to control the problem. Three weeks after Yang Yongxin's name appeared in *Science*, the Ministry of

Health issued a notification to the local government to cease any application of ECT for IA due to the lack of evidence. It furthered requested that any research should be properly registered, with informed consent from subjects and administered free of charge to participants.[40]

Three months after Deng Shensan's death, the Ministry of Health released a consultation paper called "guidance of healthy internet use for minors".[34] In response to the use of improper interventions, the paper requested the following:

1. Integrated psycho-social intervention, delivered by properly trained professionals, is encouraged.
2. Rather than complete abstinence from the internet, the goal of intervention should be the correction of psycho-behavioral problems, promotion of healthy internet use, and improvement in social functioning.
3. Confinement and physical punishment are strictly prohibited.
4. Psychiatric drugs may only be prescribed for properly diagnosed mental conditions, such as anxiety, depression and compulsive behavior. Invasive surgical procedure is strictly prohibited.

Although these guidelines sound promising, the effects were very limited. One still easily finds the advertisement of military boot camp-style "IA schools" on the web. In June 2010, 14 young people tied up a training officer and escaped from an IA centre in Jiangxu when they could no longer endure the military training. Although Yang's ECT machine had been removed by the authorities after being banned by the Ministry of Health, it was soon replaced by what he called "low frequency pulse therapy". Those youths who experienced both therapies reported that the new treatment was even more intolerable than the old electroconvulsive therapy. [41]

CONCLUSION

Even though IA has been prominent in the media for over a decade, the nature of IA has remained a controversial topic even among experts. Neither a consensus definition nor effective treatment recommendations appear to be on the near-term horizon in China, Concrete actions to reduce the societal problem of pathological internet use have not been implemented. Hence, the existing knowledge gap has led to questionable practices as well as the proliferation of financially-driven opportunities on this landscape.

The prevalence of unscientific and inhumane approaches to treat IA was deeply related to political and socio-economic problem in China. The government's political concern over internet use as a powerful and speedy medium of information exchange has added to their concerns of youth internet addiction. IA treatment centres were lucrative opportunities that benefited from China's explosive economic growth. IA treatment provided a huge profit margin to the therapists, entrepreneurs and local government officials. At the same time, the high academic expectations of parents on their only child and the lack of legal consciousness has exacerbated this complex social problem.

Many research studies in China and internationally have linked pathological use of internet with a multitude of psycho-social problems which affect one's study, work and interpersonal relationships. In South Korea, for example, it was estimated that 2.1% of children and adolescents (aged 6–19) required IA treatment, of which most might need psychotropic medications. [4] With the continuous expansion and aging of the cyber population, it is likely that more people will be suffering from IA and the problem will also affect the population other than students. Although China's internet addition problem is quite unique and extreme, its example demonstrates that the continuous lack of consensus on IA poses a barrier for those in need of proper therapy while putting non-pathological users at risk for inappropriate treatment due to societal prejudices. Standardizing a rigorous, and evidence-based definition and treatment for IA is a pressing and high priority task for contemporary public health workers.

References

[1] Asia Internet Usage Stats and Population Statistics. *Internet World Stats*. 2010. http://www.internetworldstats.com/stats3.htm#asia. Accessed July 13, 2010.

[2] Statistical Reports. *China Internet Network Information Center*. [in Chinese] 2010. http://research.cnnic.cn/html/index_81.html. Accessed July 13, 2010.

[3] Young K. Internet Addiction: The Emergence of a New Clinical Disorder. *CyberPsychology and Behavior*. 1998, 1:237-244.

[4] Block J. Issues for DSM-V: Internet Addiction. *The American Journal of Psychiatry*. 2008, 165:306-307.
[5] Pies R. Should DSM-V Designate "Internet Addiction" a Mental Disorder? *Psychiatry (Edgmont)*. 2009, 6:31-37.
[6] Substance-Related Disorders. *American Psychiatric Association DSM-5 Development*. 2010. http://www.dsm5.org/ProposedRevisions/Pages/Substance-RelatedDisorders.aspx. Accessed July 13, 2010.
[7] Chou C, Condron L, Belland J. A review of the research on internet addiction. *Educational Psychology Review*. 2005, 17:363-388.
[8] Widyanto L, Griffiths M. 'Internet Addiction': A Critical Review. *International Journal of Mental Health and Addiction*. 2005, 4:31-51.
[9] Patent application (200610138322.8): A drug for internet addiction treatment. *State Intellectual Property Office*. [in Chinese] 2006. http://search.sipo.gov.cn/sipo/zljs/hyjs-yx-new.jsp?recid=CN200610138322.8andleixin=fmzl . Accessed July 13, 2010
[10] The chaotic five years of internet addiction treatment. *Nan Fang Daily*. [in Chinese] 2009. http://nf.nfdaily.cn/nanfangdaily/nfzm/200909030126.asp . Accessed July 13, 2010
[11] Ecosystem of an internet addiction treatment centre. *China Youth On Line*. [in Chinese] 2009. http://zqb.cyol.com/content/2009-05/07/content_2655346.htm. Accessed July 13, 2010
[12] Stone R. China Reins in Wilder Impulses in Treatment of 'Internet Addiction'. *Science*. 2009, 324:1630-1631.
[13] Revisiting Yang's IA centre. *Southern People Weekly* [in Chinese] 2009. http://tech.qq.com/a/20090525/000061.htm . Accessed July 13, 2010
[14] Treating internet addiction. *News Probe*. [video in Chinese] 2009. http://space.tv.cctv.com/video/VIDE1250349298689885. Accessed July 13, 2010
[15] Chinese teenager beaten to death in internet addiction clinic. *Times Online*. 2009. http://www.timesonline.co.uk/tol/news/world/asia/article6739615.ece . Accessed July 13, 2010
[16] The Guangxi police announced cause of death of the "net addicted juvenile". *China News Service*. [in Chinese] 2009. http://www.chinanews.com.cn/gn/news/2009/08-18/1824138.shtml. Accessed July 13, 2010
[17] Four training officers are charged for beating the net addicted juvenile to death. *Southern Metropolis Daily*. [in Chinese] 2010. http://epaper.

oeeee.com/A/html/2010-02/02/content_1006785.htm. Accessed July 13, 2010

[18] Four training officers are sentenced for 2 to 10 years. *Xin Kuai Bao*. [in Chinese] 2010. http://news.xkb.com.cn/zhongguo/2010/0517/63736.html. Accessed July 13, 2010

[19] My life in "Internet addiction concentration camp". *China Youth On Line*. [in Chinese] 2009. http://zqb.cyol.com/content/2009-08/07/content_2793216.htm. Accessed July 13, 2010

[20] "That night, I jumped out of the IA centre". *China Youth On Line*. [in Chinese] 2009. http://zqb.cyol.com/content/2009-08/13/content_ 2802571.htm . Accessed July 13, 2010

[21] Treating IA with medicine in Ningbo. *Jin Ri Zao Bao* . [in Chinese] 2004. http://news.sohu.com/20041202/n223285914.shtml . Accessed July 13, 2010

[22] GoDaddy plans to stop China domain registrations. *Reuters*. 2010. http://www.reuters.com/article/idUSTRE62N5M720100324. Accessed July 13, 2010

[23] "strengthening and improving the work on minor's mind". *The Central People's Government*. 2004. http://www.gov.cn/ztzl/61/content_627824.htm. Accessed July 13, 2010

[24] The launch of "Healthy internet use and refusing addiction – a movement to treat internet addiction among minors". *Chinese Communist Youth League*. [in Chinese] 2005. http://www.ccyl. org.cn/documents/zqlf/200703/t20070321_14533.htm. Accessed July 13, 2010

[25] More than 100 cyber cafes closed during examination. *New Legal Report*. [in Chinese] 2010. http://jxfzb.jxnews.com.cn/system/ 2010/05/28/011392756.shtml . Accessed July 13, 2010

[26] China backs down over controversial censorship software. *Guardian*. 2009. http://www.guardian . Accessed July 13, 2010

[27] Byun S, Ruffini C, Mills JE, Douglas AC, Niang M, Stepchenkova S, Lee SK, Loutfi J, Lee JK, Atallah M, Blanton M. Internet addiction: metasynthesis of 1996-2006 quantitative research. *Cyberpsychol Behav*. 2009, 12:203-207.

[28] Zhang L, Ji C, Hung L. Prevalence of internet addiction and the purpose of their internet use among urban idle school students in China [in Chinese]. *Chin. J. Sch. Health*. 2009, 30:106-108.

[29] Widyanto L, McMurran M. The psychometric properties of the internet addiction test. *Cyberpsychol. Behav.* 2004, 7:443-450.
[30] Luo H, Peng Y. Relationship of internet addiction and family environment and attachment of the youth. (in Chinese) *Chinese Journal of Clinical Psychology.* 2008, 16:319-321.
[31] Ko C, Yen J, Yen C, Chen C, Yen C, Chen S. Screening for Internet addiction: an empirical study on cut-off points for the Chen Internet Addiction Scale. *Kaohsiung Journal of Medical Sciences.* 2005, 21:545-551.
[32] Bai Y, Fan F. A Study on the Internet Dependence of College Students: the Revising and Applying of a Measurement [in Chinese]. *Psychological Development and Education.* 2005, 4:99-104.
[33] China issues first definition of internet addiction. *China Daily.* 2008. http://www.chinadaily.com.cn/china/2008-11/10/content_7190091.htm . Accessed July 13, 2010
[34] Tao R, Huang X, Wang J, Zhang H, Zhang Y, Li M. Proposed diagnostic criteria for internet addiction. *Addiction.* 2010, 105:556-564.
[35] Who establish the standard of internet addiction? *China Youth On Line.* [in Chinese] 2008. http://zqb.cyol.com/content/2008-11/21/content_2440056.htm. Accessed July 13, 2010
[36] Guidance of healthy internet use for minors (consultation paper). *Ministry of Health.* [in Chinese] 2009. http://www.moh.gov.cn/publicfiles/business/htmlfiles/mohjbyfkzj/s5889/200911/44359.htm. Accessed July 13, 2010
[37] Young net addicts become "money growing tree". *Economy 30 Minutes.* [video in Chinese] 2009. http://space.tv.cctv.com/video/VIDE 1251041725842888. Accessed July 13, 2010
[38] Lessons to Learn on Education Reform. *China Internet Information Center.* 2003. http://www.china.org.cn/english/culture . Accessed July 13, 2010
[39] China's 'perfect child' generation. *BBC News.* 2007. http://news.bbc.co.uk/2/hi/asia-pacific/7001561.stm . Accessed July 13, 2010
[40] Ceasing the clinical use of ECT on treating internet addication. *Ministry of Health.* [in Chinese] 2009. http://www.moh.gov.cn/publicfiles/business/htmlfiles/mohyzs/s3586/200907/41730.htm . Accessed July 13, 2010

[41] New weapon in Yang's IA centre. *IT Times*. 2009. [in Chinese] http://www.it-times.com.cn/view_aticle.asp?classid=0andcatalogsid=1andnewsid=4470 . Accessed July 13, 2010

In: Internet Addiction
Editor: Hannah O. Price
ISBN 978-1-61122-058-2

Chapter 6

PHENOMENOLOGY OF INTERNET ADDICTION*

Caroline Gresle and Michel Lejoyeux[1]
Department of Psychiatry. Hopital Bichat-Claude Bernard, AP-HP, Paris, France

INTRODUCTION

Internet is one of the major inventions of 20th century. For most users, Internet is at the same time a way of communication, a convivial and powerful workspace and a recreational activity. Internet therefore became essential to the daily lives of more than one billion people [1]. In 1982, the word *Internet* made its appearance and the web became accessible to the public in the 90's. Its almost unlimited possibilities, in the field of the communication and the diffusion of knowledge, make it a very popular tool. Internet quickly rapidely became essential in the professional sphere as a powerful tool of transferring and sharing data and in the privacy of homes as an essential need to open up to the world and knowledge. A majority of specialists estimates that between 6%

* A version of this chapter was also published in *Peer-to-Peer Networks and Internet Policies,* edited by Diego Vegros and Jaime Saenz, published by Nova Science Publishers, Inc. It was submitted for appropriate modifications in an effort to encourage wider dissemination of research.

[1]Corresponding Author : Michel Lejoyeux. Department of Psychiatry. AP-HP, Hopital Bichat Claude Bernard. 75 877 Paris Cedex 18 and Hôpital Maison Blanche. France. Phone : 33 1 40 25 82 62. Fax : 33 1 40 25 67 80. E-mail : michel.lejoyeux@bch.aphp.fr.

and 8% of Internet users would be dependent. Nevertheless, as the phenomenon is still too recent, the national and world prevalence of cyber addiction still seems difficult to quantify [2].

Whereas the benefits are undeniable, some people to suffer the consequences of excessive use. This problem is often underestimated but some of them swear by the web. These compulsive Internet users can be described as "'connection addicts'". Their abusive use of Internet is at the origin of a new disease called the cyber addiction. Other subjects do not have an addictive relation to the web but suffer from an excessive involvement in the cyber life. They reduce their interest for relations in the "real world" and prefer on-line activities. Their abuse of the web leads them to a new form of "cocooning". Cocooning can be described as the feeling of being so well at home that one hardly wants to go out even for vital needs.

Since the 80's, psychologists have warned that fragile consumers could substitute reality for the virtual world of Internet. With the help of psychiatrists and sociologists, they tried to describe as precisely as possible this new form of dependence and to understand its implications. In 1995, Ivan Goldberg was the first to suggest the term of Internet addiction. It draws a descriptive picture of the disorder of Internet addiction based on the DSM-IV-R criteria for alcohol or drug dependence. The expression was used again in 1996 by the psychologist Kimberley Young, during a conference of the American Psychological Association in Toronto. As a pioneer of this new field of addiction, she defined Internet addiction by borrowing the criteria used for compulsive gambling [3, 4]. Her definition was to be widely used in future literature.

Cyber addiction shares some characteristics with the other forms of dependence i.e. loss of control, inability to reduce addictive consumption and feeling of intense pleasure. The criteria proposed for cyber addiction are [4, 5]:

- *Excessive use* of Internet, often associated with a loss of the sense of time,
- *A feeling of craving* when connection is stopped,
- *Withdrawal symptoms*, with a feeling of tension and/or depression
- A phenomena of *tolerance*, which tends to increase connection time even more.
- *Relapse*, a tendency for earlier patterns of earlier addictive activity to recur.

This new form of dependency has taken various names: cyber addiction, addiction to Internet, pathological or problematic use of Internet, etc. Whatever word is employed, the definition is the same: it corresponds to a relation of dependency on computers and Internet. By extension, it involves a dependency on network games, chat rooms, on-line pathological gambling or compulsive buying on web sites devoted to buying.

PREVALENCE, RISK FACTORS AND PSYCHIATRIC CO-MORBIDITIES

Prevalence

In 1998, Young estimated that between 5 and 10% of Net surfers show Internet dependency. One year later, a large survey on this topic, coordinated by David Greenfield estimated that 6% of Americans are cyber addicts. Elias Aboujaoude found lower rates for prevalence of Internet addiction. He estimated that only 1% of the American population is concerned with dependence to Internet. According to Block, 9 million of Americans could be dependent on Internet or may be at risk [6]. For Block (2007) the precise evaluation of the disorder remains largely marked by a lack of data. Furthermore, he suspects a minimization of the phenomenon in the United States, caused by shame, denial and the under-recognition of the disorder and its complications [7].

Other assessments were undertaken in Asia. The majority of works were published in South Korea [7]. They suggest that this area of the world is statistically the most exposed to Internet addiction. However a number of other countries have not undertaken national studies on web addiction yet and may ignore or underestimate the impact of this addiction. Following single cases of deaths which occurred due to a prolonged and intensive use of Internet, South Korea considered that addiction to Internet was a serious public health problem. In 2006, its government estimated that approximately 210,000 children aged 6 to 19 (20.1%), were dependent or had a problematic use of Internet [7]. According to Ahn (2007), 80% of these children would need psychotropic treatment, while 20 to 24% would require hospitalization. South-Koreans students spend on average 23 hours a week on Internet games [7]. These surprising estimates are unfortunately the same as in many countries where Internet is extremely popular among young people [5, 7].

China belongs to the countries also exposed to a pathological use of Internet. As it is the most populated country in the world, it also has the greatest number of Web surfers - 298 million at the end of 2008. According to the Chinese Internet Network Information Centre, this estimate increased by approximately 42% en une année préciser SVP. Officially, Internet addiction is not recognized in China. yet [8]. In 2008, J Block, quoted Tao Ran who estimated that approximately 13.7% of Chinese teenagers were Internet dependent– i.e. 10 million.

In France, Internet met with the same scepticism concerning its addictiveness. However the number of psychiatric consultations for cyber addiction has not ceased to increase in recent years. In 2004, the phenomenon concerned 150.000 French. In 2008, A. Grossokst and P. Jeanneteau, two deputies, wrote a report to establish the extent of the problem. According to their estimates, 3 to 4% of the French (600 to 800,000 people) would be dependent on Internet via an excessive use of on-line video games. Only 10% of these Internet addicts consult a specialist. These figures are all the more overpowering, as they do not take into account the full extent of the phenomenon of cyber addiction: chat- rooms, online gambling, cyber pornography, E-mails ... More worrying still, the reported estimates mainly relate to young people aged from 13 to 25.

Risk Factors – Co-Morbidity

The pathological use of Internet is more frequent: after an early experimentation, for socially isolated and young people. Men are more exposed to Internet addiction [5, 9, 10, 11, 12,]. Yang and Tung (2004) studied the prevalence of Internet addiction in Taiwanese teenagers from 17 to 19 years. Among the addicts identified, men were overrepresented (ratio of 3 boys for 1 girl). Cao and Lu (2006) came to the same conclusion: 83% of Chinese teenage cyber addicts were boys versus 11% of girls. If most studies seem to agree on the relationship between gender and the risk for Internet addiction, few works have found no relationship between gender and web addiction [13].

Interpersonal factors are important for initiation of Internet dependence. Psychiatric disorders increase the risk for Internet addiction. Web surfers having a predisposition to mood disorders [5, 14], anxiety - social phobia – [5, 15], depression [5, 14, 15, 16,] or low self-esteem [5, 15], are more at the risk to develop cyber addiction. Links between suicide and Internet addiction were also shown. Among cyberaddicts, this last correlation is more important in girls [15].

Conversely, the mode of use of Internet seems predictive of Internet dependence [5, 12]. Subjects using Internet for its social functions are more exposed to addiction [5, 12]. Web surfers at risk for dependence mainly use Internet to meet people [17] and spend more and more time on these sites to maintain these numerous virtual relationships.

Many complications affect consumers who misuse Internet. Most frequent damages include sleep and sight problems [15], migraines, back and cervical pains and carpal tunnel syndrome. Sleep is disturbed and can no longer play its repairing role. The pathological use of Internet is also marked by food disorders [4], lack of hygiene and in the most extreme cases, death [7]. On a psychological level, one finds, a reduced interest in everything with does not concern the object of dependence. The importance attached to Internet influences almost all thoughts of the users who misuse it. It causes anxiety and maladaptive cognitions according Davis (2001) [18]. In this article, Davis was tracked it two types: thought about the self of the kind "I am only good on the internet" and thought about the world of the style "Internet is the only place I am respected" This exclusiveness influences the feelings and attitudes by altering, for example, the initiation of behaviours related to socialisation [16]. This involves an impoverishment of affective life, both relational and intellectual [16]. Addicts have numerous problems in daily life [5]. They neglect family and friends and spend more time connected to internet than in "real" life [15]. Addicts can be more inclined to divorce, lose their employment more easily, encounter educational difficulties and give up school or university.

Treatments for Cyber Addiction

The treatment of cyber addicts calls principally upon psychotherapeutic treatments which can be supplemented by pharmacological treatments. In most cases, cyber addiction is treated only with psychotherapy. In the same way as with other addictive disorders, motivational counselling is an essential precondition which aims at initiating behavioural change by helping the patients to solve their problems and to explore their ambivalence. Before undertaking any therapy, it is necessary to inform the patients about the pathological use of Internet, to give him a definition and to outline consequences of the disorder. Above all, it is essential to alert patients of the addictive characteristic of their behaviour. Like in almost all other forms of addiction, the most difficult stage for success remains the recognition of the dependence.

Among the therapies used, that of psycho-analytical inspiration seems most adapted in the getting cyber addicts to assume responsibility. They mainly use verbal language in order to rehabilitate the expressive function of thought. Cyber addicts do not lack the capacity to think but they lack the capacity to express themselves.

Support therapies: The cyber addict learns how to manage his behaviour by becoming aware of factors which make him an addict. Among these therapies: "Web counselling" is a kind of virtual clinic and group therapies. There are also Internet Relay Chat Rooms (IRC), developed by ex-cyber addicts or their entourage. Particularly developed in the US these help-lines facilitate verbal expression and then later encourage the cyber addict to engage in "a true" dialogue face-to-face. Groups of mutual aid, like Anonymous Net surfers, copied the therapeutic program developed by Alcoholics Anonymous which includes twelve stages. In these groups, the addict admits the reality of his addiction to Internet.

Cognitive and behavioural therapies have also been offered to web addicts. Cognitive-behavioural model of cyber addiction highlights the role of unsuited cognitions and dysfunctional behaviour [18]. It identifies two types of unsuited cognitions specific to the individuals having a problematic use of Internet: erroneous cognitions about the patient and of the world around him. Among false cognitions reported by Davis can be found: "I am weak when I am not connected, but online I am somebody"; "I am a failure when I am not connected" [18]. Goal of the cognitive treatments includes a cognitive reorganisation of these distorted thoughts. This work supposes that the patient recognizes his false cognitions and accepts to cure them [18, 19]. False cognitive distortions are associated with addictive behaviours. Other behavioural approachs can be offer to web addicts are: techniques of relaxation, keeping a diary which evaluates automatic thoughts. *Behavioral Approach* [18, 19], aims at a tangible modification of relation to the web.

Several techniques are reported such as:

- modifying the sighting of the computer,
- changing times of connections,
- practising activities incompatible with Internet,
- learn relaxation.

The patient is encouraged to practice activities unrelated to Internet such as sport, socialising, cultural activities or hobbies, outings during the week.

PREVENTION OF INTERNET ADDICTION

The cyber addiction is a true society' problem whose frightening consequences led many countries to work out a prevention of the risks. Among the projects of prevention in progress, can be cited the publicity campaigns informing on French television on the dangers of Internet. Even if they do not immediately target the problem of cyber addiction, these campaigns have the merit to alert parents on the unsuited contents that circulate on the web for their children and teenagers. These spots which put in scene a mother opening her front door and inviting in avatars of violence (Skinheads, destroying robots), or in an other one, avatars of pornography and paedophilia, conclude on these words: "don't let danger come in your home!". These campaigns are interesting insofar as they really say something to the parents and the families on the danger that Internet's contents can represent. By alienating a parental control on the contents diffused by Internet, the parents keep an eye on what their children use Internet for.

Public awareness campaigns on the addictive use of Internet should be carried out in the next years. They aim at informing the adults on the phenomenon of cyber addiction, knowing the risks and locating the symptoms. In parallel, prevention campaigns early targeting young people may inform them on the dangers of a too regular use of Internet and video games.

Beginning again what had been made already elsewhere as regards prevention against the dangers of alcohol, one will find in the commercials the diffusion of medical messages. These messages will informe on the dangers of an intensive use of any support related to data processing, Internet or video games. Such as for the anti-tobacco campaigns, of the warning messages, as "an excessive use is harmful for health" or "to play takes time", would come to supplement the descriptive PEGI (Side-European Range Information) on packing of any data-processing apparatus: computers, consoles, video games…

Within the framework of a more active prevention, it is planned to interfere directly on the game itself in various ways:

- A visible clock on the screens would indicate the time spent in front of a game and could even flicker after three to four hours of consecutive play. It would be relayed by warning messages posted regularly beyond excessive time of use of the game.
- A non playable psychological character is also considered. He would intervene in the game to< invite the player to make a pause or to encourage it to reflect over time that he passes on the game.
- Another more active measurement would consist in tiring the avatars of the players by reducing their power and thus obliging the players to make a pause long enough in the game in order to restore the energy of their character.

Conclusion

Internet is an incontestably amazing communication tool that is bound to occupy an increasingly dominating place in our lives. It is important that all the protagonists, Net surfers, doctors, psychologists, legislators, become aware of the potential dangers that can involve cyber-dependency. Far from demonising the use, it appears necessary today to take the measurement of the drifts which result from this.

References

[1] Internet World Stats. http://www.internetworldstats.com/stats.htm , view on the January 27th 2009.

[2] Dell'Osso, B., Altamura, A., Allen, Marazziti, D., and Hollander, E. (2006). Epidemiologic and clinical updates on impulse control disorders: A critical review. *European Archives of Psychiatry and Clinical Neuroscience*, 256, 464-475.

[3] Young, K., (1996). Psychology computer use: XL. Addictive use of the internet: a case that breaks the stereotype. *Psychological Rep.,* 79, 899-902.

[4] Young, K., (1998). Caught in the Net: How to Recognize the Signs of Internet Addiction -- and A Winning Strategy For Recovery, Wiley, New York.

[5] Yang, S. and Tung, C. (2007). Comparison of Internet addicts and non-addicts in Taiwanese high school. *Computer in Human Behavior*, 23 (1), 79-96

[6] J., Fitzgerald (2008). Internet Addiction: Recognition and Interventions. *Archives of Psychiatric Nursing*, Vol.22, N°2.

[7] Block, J., (2008). Issue for DSM-V: Internet Addiction, American *Journal of Psychiatry*, mars, 165-3.

[8] Wu, H. and Zhu, K. (2004) Path analysis on related factors causing internet addiction disorder in college students. *Chinese Journal of Public Health*, 20, 1363-1634.

[9] Morahan-Martin, J. and Schumacher, P., (2000). Incidence and correlates of pathological internet uses among college students, *Computer in Human Behavior*, 16, 13-29.

[10] Wang, W., (2001). Internet dependency and psychosocial maturity among college students, *International Journal of Human-Computer Studies*, 55, 919-938

[11] Cao, F. and Su, L. (2006). Internet addiction among Chinese adolescents: prevalence and psychological features. *Child: care, health and development.* 33, 3, 275-281.

[12] Li, S. and Chung, T. (2006). Internet function and Internet addictive behaviour. *Computer in human Behavior*, 22, 1067-1071.

[13] Hall, A. andParsons, J. (2001). Internet addiction: College case study using vest practices in cognitive behavior Therapy. *Journal of mental Health Counseling*, 23(4), 312-328.

[14] Shapira, N., Goldsmith, T., Keck, P., Khosla, U. and Mc Elroy, S. (2000). Psychiatry features of individuals with problematic internet use. *Journal of Affective Disorders*, 57, 267-272.

[15] Kim, K., Ryu, E., Chon, M., Yeun, E., Choi, S., Seo, J., and Nam, B., (2005). Internet addiction in Korean adolescents and its relation to depression and suicidal ideation: A questionnaire survey. *International journal of nursing studies*, 43(2), 185-192

[16] Baruch, Y. (2001). The autistic society. *Information and management,* 38, 129-136.

[17] Ju, M. (2000). Research on personal characteristics, the behavior of using Internet and Internet addiction for Taiwanese college study. Master thesis. Taiwan.

[18] Davis, R. (2001). A cognitive-behavioral model of pathological Internet use. *Computer in Human Behavior*, 17; 187-195.

[19] Caplan, S. (2002). Problematic Internet use ad psychosocial well-being: development of theory-bases cognitive-behavioral measurement instrument. *Computer in Human Behavior*, 18; 553-575.

In: Internet Addiction
Editor: Hannah O. Price
ISBN 978-1-61122-058-2

Chapter 7

INTERNET ADDICTION IN CHILDREN AND ADOLESCENTS[*]

Keith W. Beard
Marshall University, Huntington, West Virginia, USA

ABSTRACT

The creation of the Internet has had several positive and negative results on the world. Additionally, certain aspects of the Internet make it a unique medium of communication with its own set of norms, standards, language, etc. These various factors have influenced children and adolescents. Problematic Internet use, which has become known as Internet addiction, is not limited by demographic elements. However, there may be certain factors about this medium that could make children and adolescents vulnerable to using the Internet in a dysfunctional way. These factors are examined. Additionally, special considerations and treatment options are reviewed for mental health professionals who treat children and adolescents for their problematic Internet use. Future research on particular aspects of problematic Internet use with children and adolescents is suggested.

---

[*] A version of this chapter was also published in *Computer Science Research Trends,* edited by Casey B. Yarnell, published by Nova Science Publishers, Inc. It was submitted for appropriate modifications in an effort to encourage wider dissemination of research.

THE IMPACT OF THE INTERNET

The development of the Internet has had a very positive influence for many people. Economically, the Internet has provided business and financial opportunities (Beard, 2002). Socially, users are able to meet others similar to them and foster favorable impressions. The Internet allows people to make friends, maintain relationships, play games, gain emotional support, and learn about other cultures (McNamee, 1996; Parks and Floyd, 1996; Scherer, 1997). With regard the physical and mental health, using the Internet may provide relief from anxiety and depression by acting as an escape or helping the person gain needed support and education about their problem (Armstrong, Phillips, and Saling, 2000; Harmon, 1998; Kraut et al., 1998; Pocius, 1991; Shotton, 1989; Suler, 1996a; Young, 1996b, 1997, 1998b). It has even been suggested that the Internet has increased the self-concept that some people hold about themselves. Shotton (1989) described how the Internet has allowed those who are knowledgeable in the computing market to offer advice to those less knowledgeable. This has resulted in higher self-esteem and self-confidence, and improved self-concept for those helping others. Computer and Internet use have also allowed people to increase their knowledge about various related technologies. It has been suggested that there has been an improvement in writing abilities and intellectual growth for some people as a result of their computer and Internet use.

In contrast, the Internet may have created a new set of difficulties for the general population. Several studies have illustrated that there are a significant number of people who report averse consequences from their Internet use (Coopers, Griffin-Shelley, and Delmonico, 2001; Young, 1997, 1998a, 1998b). Researchers (Stern, 1999; Winn, 1985; Young, 1998b) have compared the introduction of the Internet to the introduction of the television when identifying potential negative impacts. It was initially thought that the television would bring families together. Griffiths (1997) and Winn (1985) claim that the television has separated families. In the same way, the Internet is providing a backdrop for several critical family problems (Oravec, 2000). Griffiths (1997) and Winn (1985) go on by stating that even though families are spending time together watching television, their interaction is minimal and quality time may now be consumed by television viewing. Like television, the Internet may contribute to decreased family interaction. Television has also allowed families to avoid confronting their problems which then grow and become more difficult to resolve. The researchers go so far as to claim that television has played an important role in the disintegration of the family.

Also, like television, the Internet can be detrimental to physical development and growth by limiting activity. Pike (1999) goes on to compare these two mediums. She characterizes the Internet as television on steroids. However, the difference is that television shows end where as the Internet provides a sense of "boundarylessness" that can be enticing to a person.

Beard (2002) states that another negative consequence of the Internet has to do with the content that is obtained. For example, there is an abundance of misinformation that can be perpetuated. It can be difficult to obtain desired information because of the numerous web sites that have to be reviewed and sorted through in order to find the desired material. Other issues with the content on the Internet include the fact that people have more access to pornographic material. This has lead to some people being fired from their jobs and conflict in relationships. Dangerous information can be obtained from the Internet such as instructions for how to make a bomb out of common household items.

Negative consequences with interpersonal relationships can occur as a result of Internet use. People can create new identities or misrepresent themselves (McCormick and McCormick, 1992). Adolescents may be particularly susceptible to this behavior since they are often unhappy with their appearance and are involved with the developmental task of integrating various roles into a unified identity. As a result, this misrepresentation can cause disappointment if a pen-pal is never met or there is disappointment after he/she was met (Turkle, 1996). Another dangerous misinterpretation of identity can occur as a result of sexual predators easily soliciting large numbers of children and adolescents in a relatively anonymous environment (Dombrowski, LeMasney, and Ahia, 2004). Armstrong et al. (2000) and Young (1995, 1996b, 1998a, 1998b) report other interpersonal relationship issues such as less time is spent with people in the user's life resulting in impatience, arguments, and a strain in the relationship. A person's school work, extracurricular activities, or after-school employment may suffer if too much time is spent scanning the Internet. The Internet may also contribute to people escaping from social interactions and hinder the development of social skills (Beard and Wolf, 2000).

Young (1995, 1998b) described how schools are rushing to add Internet access for students. There is an underlying belief that children need Internet access in order to stay competitive in the global marketplace. However, one survey (Barber, 1997) revealed that 86 percent of responding teachers, librarians, and computer coordinators did not believe that Internet use improved classroom performance. These respondents claim that the Internet is too disorganized and unrelated to the school curriculum. Not only can inaccurate information be perpetuated quickly but much of the information is unattainable (McCormick and McCormick, 1992; Turkle, 1996). Only 9 percent of the estimated 800 million web pages are covered by the top 11 search engines ("Search Engines," 1999). Schools have cut funding for programs in the creative arts and invest the money in a technology that may not provide benefits to the students (Young, 1995, 1998b).

The Internet Culture

There may be qualities with this medium of communication that have allowed an Internet culture to develop. The Internet culture has its own set of values, standards, language, signs, and artifacts (Beard and Wolf, 2000; Correll, 1995; Friess, 1998; Griffiths, 2001; Parks and Floyd, 1996; Suler, 1996b; Young, 1997, 1998a). Symbols and initials have been given meanings. For example, "LOL" stands for "Laugh Out Loud," "IMHO" stands for "In My Humble Opinion," and ":-P" represents "I'm sticking my tongue out" (Friess, 1998). The exchange of these standards and signs can express deep meaning and psychological bonds may develop quickly (Correll, 1995; Kiesler et al., 1984; Suler, 1996b; Young, 1997, 1998a). The person reading the symbols is able to create in the writer what their ideal person would be but this creation is based only on words.

For many, the main attraction to the Internet is the anonymity (Correll, 1995; Griffiths, 1997; Kiesler, et al., 1984; Young, 1997, 1998a, 1998b). Unlike face-to-face communication, demographics have to be announced in order to be known (Correll, 1995). Many Internet users take on different personas when on-line (Kandell, 1998; Suler, 1996b; Young, 1997, 1998a, 1998b). Users may change their persona and create different profile information about themselves depending on their mood or desires. As mentioned previously, this may be particularly attractive for adolescents as they go through some of the development tasks associated with this period. An identity crisis can occur as adolescents begin to integrate various roles into a solid identity. Questions may develop such as, “Who am I?” or “What am I going to be?” This aspect of the Internet and the factors associated with identity development may join to provide adolescents with an opportunity to “try on” different identities and determine what “fits” for them. Young (1997, 1998a, 1998b) found that some users chose identities that were an ideal self that represented the opposite of what the person is in real life. As a result, the chosen persona is a way to fulfill unmet needs. Others chose a persona that represented an emotion or trait that may be repressed. Some users even take on a different gender, age, or race. The impact of taking on a different persona for adolescents, and those interacting with that person, needs to be studied further.

King (1996) and Young (1997, 1998a, 1998b) believe that Internet users tend to take more emotional risks and may express opinions on-line that they are unable to express to others in the real world. This creates a deep need to continue these bonds and receive the support that they are lacking in the real world. Adolescents may be particularly vulnerable because they often feel isolated. As a result, these bonds made over the Internet may take on even more significance in the adolescent's life. However, the commitment of friends on the Internet can be ended with the simple click of a button. The Internet offers the illusion of companionship without the demands often placed on friendships. Interestingly, even though people were more embarrassed about meeting face-to-face after interacting via the Internet, they actually reported liking each other better (Correll, 1995; Kiesler, et al., 1984). Kiesler and colleagues (1984) specifically address this social psychology aspect of electronic communication in the results of their study which explored the physiological arousal and affective consequences of computer communication. Results suggested that computer-mediated communication is not physiologically arousing. However, there can be affective consequences with computer-mediated versus face-to-face communication when people are getting to know each other. Affective consequences include changes in emotionality, interpersonal attraction, responsiveness to others, and self-disclosure.

Users are not shy to express positive and negative feedback to those they communicate within this forum. It is not unusual in this culture to ask personal questions upon the first on-line meeting between two users (Kandell, 1998; King, 1996; Suler, 1996b; Young, 1997, 1998a). The lack of face-to-face communication may also create a feeling of safety and encourage more flirtation and overtures of friendship (Harmon, 1998; McCormick and McCormick, 1992; Morahan-Martin and Schumacher, 2000; Suler, 1996b).

Young (1997, 1998a, 1998b) explains that the Internet environment allows for any virtual experience. If the person desired to hurt his or her teacher, the person can go into a Multi-User Dungeons and Dragons (MUDS) or on-line gaming site and blow up an enemy. If the person fantasized of ripping off the clothes of an attractive man or woman it can be simulated in a cybersex encounter. If the person wanted to know what it would be like to be bisexual, the person can go on-line and engage in a fantasy. Once these unconscious drives are brought to the conscious mind it becomes difficult to suppress them again. As a result, the Internet user may begin to blur the distinction between their real-world personality and their on-line persona.

PROBLEMATIC USE OF THE INTERNET

Beard and Wolf (2000) believe that problematic Internet use can be found in any age, social, educational, and economic range. Excessive Internet users have been called Internet addicts, pathological Internet users, computer addicts, computer mediated communication addicts, and computer junkies. The term that has been most often used for problematic Internet use is "Internet addiction." This includes a mixture of obsessive-like characteristics and impulse control problems related to a person's Internet usage resulting in a preference for on-line rather than in-person interactions (Beard and Wolf, 2000; Pratarelli, Browne, and Johnson, 1999). Each of the previously listed terms reflects a different understanding of the nature of excessive Internet use. The most popular term utilized is "Internet addiction." While this term will be used throughout this chapter, it is my position that this term does not accurately reflect the phenomenon of excessive Internet use. While there are commonalities between excessive Internet use and an addiction, excessive Internet use does not result in all of the symptoms and behaviors associated with a chemical addiction, such as physical withdrawal. Moreover, comparison of excessive Internet use with pathological gambling suggests that this behavior with the Internet may be better classified as an impulse control disorder rather than an addiction (Beard and Wolf, 2000; Young, 1998b). Given the issues outlined above, terms such as excessive, problematic, or maladaptive Internet use are most optimal for describing this behavior as they involve fewer theoretical overtones than terms such as "Internet addiction."

Media attention has stereotyped those who are Internet addicted as predominantly young/adolescent, introverted, and computer-oriented males (Scherer, 1997; Young, 1996a, 1998a). While this stereotype may have been true in the past (Pocius, 1991), the availability of computers and the easy access for everyone to the Internet is quickly challenging this notion and causing researchers to re-assess their previous conceptualizations of what characteristics a person addicted to the Internet may possess (Armstrong et al., 2000). Now, most Internet users are young students (Treuer, Fabian, and Furedi, 2001). Young's (1998b) findings demonstrated that the number of male and female computer and Internet users may be changing. She reported that 61 percent of her respondents were women. It is suspected that the change in Internet use is related to the availability of this technology.

Subjects, who completed a survey posted on the Internet and met a proposed criteria for problematic Internet use (Young, 1995, 1996b, 1998a, 1998b), described their personality as bold, outgoing, open-minded, and assertive. Many of the Internet users reported being depressed, lonely, having low self-esteem, and anxiety. Pathological Internet users typically score higher on loneliness scales than non-pathological Internet users (Morahan-Martin and Schumacher, 2000). The Internet may provide pathological users with a way to express themselves that is considered more satisfying than previous coping skills. Other common personality characteristics included having pride in their intellect, and the use of the defense mechanism called intellectualization (Correll, 1995; Pocius, 1991; Shotton, 1989).

New users could be more vulnerable to the development of pathological Internet use. Twenty-five percent of those who completed Young's (1996b, 1997, 1998a, 1998b) survey on the Internet reported becoming addicted to the Internet within the first six months on-line. She went on to report that 58 percent of the respondents met her criteria for Internet addiction within one year. Most felt intimidated by the computer initially but began to feel a sense of competency and exhilaration from mastering the technology and learning to navigate the applications quickly (Kandell, 1998; Kraut et al., 1998; Shotton, 1989; Young, 1996b, 1997, 1998a, 1998b).

The survey administered by Young (1996b, 1997, 1998b) also found that her addicted respondents used the Internet an average of 38 hours a week. In general, adolescents have been found to use the Internet more hours than adults (Kraut et al., 1998). Young (1998b) explains that respondents admitted to trying to cut down on their Internet use and failing despite significant problems it was causing. Nearly 80 percent of Internet addicts engage in two-way communication forums such as chat rooms and interactive games. The greater the availability of the Internet, the increased chance that people will engage in various activities offered on the Internet.

Problematic Use by Children and Adolescents

Children and adolescents are becoming active users of the Internet (Young, 1998b). It has been suggested by Young (1998b) that many parents are unaware about what their children do on the Internet. Some parents may not even know how to turn on the computer. There are parents who have banned the use of the Internet or controlled access for fear of exposing their children to pornography and contact with pedophiles that frequent sites for children and adolescents. Neither being unaware of nor prohibiting the use of the Internet will help parents confront the issues that the Internet raises concerning their children and adolescents.

Young (1998b) pointed out that students are primed for Internet access. Most are typically exposed to computer games, digital music players, cell phones, and digital cameras. If they have not already been introduced to the Internet by high school, these other technical gadgets prepared them to learn about and embrace new technology. When examining adolescents, it has been discovered that their perception of how useful the Internet is was a major variable in predicting whether an adolescent would become addicted to the Internet (Xuanhui and Gonggu, 2001).

Warning signs that give evidence that a child or teen is abusing the Internet have been suggested by Young (1998b). The child may be excessively fatigued due to a change in sleep patterns because of excessive on-line use. Academic problems may be noticed. Parents may believe that the child is spending their time on the computer working on class assignments when the child is actually on-line. A child who is dependent on the Internet typically spends more and more time on-line which results in negative ramifications on the child's daily routine, school performance, and parental relationship (Lin and Tsai, 2002). Additionally, the child may show a decline in other hobbies because the Internet becomes the only non-curricular activity. The child may withdraw from friends and make emotional attachments with those on the Internet. Adolescents who are dependent on the Internet may even go as far as believing that their excessive Internet use enhances their peer relationships (Lin and Tsai, 2002). Anger, irritability, edginess, and acting out may result from a decrease in Internet accessibility; this experience has been coined the "cybershakes" (Young, 1998b). A youth's reaction to limits being set on Internet use may provide further evidence of possible Internet addiction behaviors.

Clearly, pathological Internet use may be an indication of other underlying problems. Young (1997, 1998b) discussed how children may use the Internet to alleviate depression, anxiety, and to escape from family discord. Real-life problems return after this temporary alleviation. As a result, these problems may now be seen as even more difficult to endure. Depression, guilt, and loneliness deepen as a byproduct of excessive Internet use (Morahan-Martin, 1999). Young (1997, 1998b) continues, stating that these feelings push the person into going on-line for even longer periods of time. This same cycle is also seen in alcoholics and compulsive gamblers as they engage in their addictive behaviors.

It is normal for adolescents to be plagued with feelings of low self-esteem. Some adolescents become dependent on the social contact they receive from the Internet. Children and adolescents may be seeking out confidants on the Internet to discuss issues that they feel others in the real world, such as their parents, will not understand. Adolescents form such strong connections with others on the Internet that they often consider each other a "cyberbro" or "cybersis" (Young, 1998b).

Young (1997, 1998b) also suggested that the Internet may attract children with Attention Deficit Hyperactivity Disorder (ADHD). Those children diagnosed with ADHD may find the Internet appealing because of the abundance of stimulation and rapidly changing material.

Causes of Internet Addiction

The cause of Internet addiction is more than likely a multifaceted phenomenon (Wang, 2001). From a sociocultural stand point there may be familial, social, and cultural dynamics that prompt excessive Internet use. For example, the person may use the Internet to escape family conflict. From a social aspect, some people may lack certain social skills that would enable them to fulfill these social needs in places other than the computer. Likewise, modeling may play a role. Children and adolescents may see their primary care giver, other adults, or peers engaging the various activities and material offered on the Internet and then model that behavior. Additionally, children and adolescents can witness and experience peer pressure from those around them engaging in Internet use. There may be the expectation from friends for the Internet user to engage in various on-line activities. Likewise, cultural factors such as the push to be a "technologically advanced society" or the necessity to use the Internet for school assignments could encourage Internet use to a point that is detrimental to the person. The environment in which the Internet is being used could also increase the potential for pathological use. Using the Internet in the comfort of one's home can increase the chances that the person will not want to leave this environment.

TREATMENT CONSIDERATIONS WITH CHILDREN AND ADOLESCENTS

Marlatt (1985) feels that the focus of treatment should revolve around the assumption that people can learn effective ways to change their addictive behaviors regardless of how the problem developed. Likewise, addictive behaviors are controllable behaviors even though their cause may be determined by multiple factors. Therefore, ideal intervention programs should include behavioral, cognitive, and lifestyle changes.

When intervening with children and adolescents the therapist often works closely and intervenes with the care givers. Stanton and Heath (1997) reported how family disruptions and stress may promote the onset of addictive behavior. These same disruptions and stresses may influence how family members enable, encourage, or overlook addictive behaviors such as Internet use. Families may rationalize the pathological Internet use as a phase that will be resolved in time (Young, 1995, 1996b, 1998a). Learning ways to handle family crises and stabilizing the family are the goals. Family therapy may be a necessary treatment modality. When treating the family system, the family becomes the "client." Young (1995) suggested that the family be educated on how the Internet can be addictive. Exploration into previous family problems is needed since this may be a reason why the child or adolescent sought out the Internet and began using this technology in a maladaptive way. There should also be some effort to reduce the blame placed on the Internet addict for their behaviors. The family is also encouraged to help the Internet addicted child find new hobbies, take time for him/herself, and listen to the child's feelings. Stanton and Heath (1997) continued stating that the family has to learn how to go on with life without the use of the Internet or with specific modifications so that problematic Internet use will not recur. The family may need to be reorganized and members will be expected to take on their expected roles in the family. These roles may have shifted when the addicted person began having a problem. Care givers should be supportive but not enable excessive Internet use by aiding children with excuses for why the child missed school or failed an assignment. It is important to validate the child for any effort that is being made.

Young (1998b) suggested that a therapist assist care givers in establishing agreed upon reasonable rules and goals regarding Internet use. If there is a division regarding how to parent between the care givers, the child may use this to create an even larger divergence. Peele and Brodsky (1991) stressed to the care giver that lecturing the child is typically an ineffective and counter-productive intervention. Acknowledging and exploring reasons why the child may be using the Internet may help the parent understand the issue at hand and how to best deal with it. Young (1998b) continues, stating that the child may feel blamed or criticized for his/her Internet use. The care giver can learn how to effectively reassure the child that this is not the case and focus the concerns over specific changes such as fatigue, declining grades, and social withdrawal. It is vital that the parents are consistent with the rules that are established. The care givers should encourage other activities to fill in the time gained by decreasing Internet use.

Young (1998b) also recommended that care givers get on-line and see what their children could be exposed to on the Internet. This could also result in the care givers modeling appropriate Internet use (Peele and Brodsky, 1991). Children and adolescents can learn to emulate their parent's responses to situations such as what to do if inappropriate web sites are accessed or what to do if someone the child or adolescent does not know attempts to contact them. Care givers can also learn how to take a proactive stance and talk to children about the Internet just as they would talk to them about drugs and alcohol.

Finally, Young (1995, 1998b) suggested that families find support in groups for other addictions such as Al-Anon. Information about dealing with any addiction in the family can be obtained at these meetings. Even if the person only goes and listens to the experiences of family members of alcoholics they will see similarities in their situations, feel validated, and less alone. Parents may be able to seek support regarding their Internet addicted child from a parent's association and as a result, they may find that other parents are experiencing similar difficulties.

FUTURE RESEARCH AND CONCLUSIONS

When examining Internet addiction one factor that needs to be taken into consideration is the limited empirical research on Internet addiction. Likewise, the empirical research that has been conducted contains methodological flaws that could impact the results. Additionally, the term "Internet addiction" has been used to denote all types of abuse with a variety of Internet applications and there is a controversy over whether it should even be called an addiction (Beard, 2002; Beard and Wolf, 2000; Scherer, 1997). Some researchers (Young, Pistner, and O'Mara, 1999) have claimed that there are numerous subtypes of Internet addiction such as Cybersex, Cyber-relationships, online stock trading, information surfing, and computer games. However, even if this is the case, it is not uncommon for a single word to describe a diverse category of behavior (Jaffe, 1990).

Areas that need further exploration include prevalence rates and issues related to specific populations. There could be issues that need to be taken into account when assessing various ethnic groups, income levels, individuals with various mental disorders, and differences between adolescents and children. Walther and Reid (2000) agreed, stating that past research has ignored a broader range of participants.

Research that includes retesting participants and replication of various studies is also needed (Walther and Reid, 2000). Young (1995, 1997, 1998b) suggests that longitudinal studies of the Internet and its users be done. This may reveal certain personality traits, family dynamics, social support, or communication skills that promote Internet addictive behaviors. Additionally, there may be undiscovered differences between new and old users. Since the Internet is readily available and user-friendly, the characteristics of those who may become addicted to the Internet could be shifting.

Future research also needs to focus on what it actually is about the Internet that children and adolescents find addictive (Griffiths, 1998; King, 1996; Walther and Reid, 2000; Young, 1997, 1998b). Is it the computer? Is it the typing? Is it the information gained? Is it the anonymity? Is it the interactions with other users? Is it the types of activities in which the individual is engaged? (Beard, 2002; Beard and Wolf, 2000). Young (1996b, 1998b) makes the important point that the Internet addict may not be addicted to the Internet per se, but addicted to the application, emotional state, or mental response that is received from on-line behaviors. All of these factors could play a role in making the Internet reinforcing. Therefore, the Internet may not be addictive but how it is used may be the addictive aspect of this technology (Harmon, 1998). Additionally, it is unknown how important individual characteristics are in determining if applications are addictive (Pocius, 1991; Walther and Reid, 2000). Likewise, it is assumed that off-line activities are healthier than on-line behavior but this has not been examined (Walther and Reid, 2000).

Goolkasian (1995) and Young (1995, 1996b) recommend that those involved with youth be aware of this growing phenomenon and the role that mental health professionals and other's involved in a child's life can take with addressing Internet use and abuse. These difficulties should be examined in a proactive manner rather then waiting for the crisis to occur and then "picking up the pieces." Mental health professionals pride themselves on their ability to predict behavior. Introducing new technology and simultaneously using what we know about the mental, social, and physical aspects of people to counteract negative effects may lessen the onset of difficulties and the formation of crises.

There are millions of people on the Internet and the number keeps growing. In 2002, Neilson/NetRatings report that over 422 million people in 21 countries had access to the Internet in their homes (Mariano, 2002) with each U.S. citizens averaging 35 on-line visits in one month from their home computers in 2007 (Nelison/NetRatings, 2007). Since the concept of Internet addiction is a new phenomenon, mental health professionals and school counselors need to be alerted to the fact that many individuals may be reluctant to seek treatment believing that the clinician will not take their difficulties seriously. Keeping an open mind that there could be problems with how some children and adolescents use the Internet, trying to understand why this technology is used in a maladaptive way, and recognizing the signs and symptoms of Internet addiction will be beneficial for all of those involved.

The continuing debate over the existence of Internet addiction will probably go on for some time. Regardless of whether or not the term Internet addiction is used, there are children and adolescents who are developing a harmful dependence on the Internet. Anything can become addictive when it becomes obsessive (Walther and Reid, 2000). Regardless of whether this problematic behavior is a result of the Internet itself or some other factor, there is a problem in how some children and adolescents use the Internet and steps need to be taken to help these individuals.

REFERENCES

Armstrong, L., Phillips, J. G., and Saling, L. L. (2000). Potential determinants of heavier Internet usage. *International Journal of Human-Computer Studies*, 53, 537-550,

Barber, A. (1997, March 11). Net's educational value questioned. USA Today. pp. 4D.

Beard, K. W. (2002). Internet addiction: Current status and implications for employees. *Journal of Employment Counseling*, 39, 2-11.

Beard, K. W., and Wolf, E. M. (2001). Modification in the proposed diagnostic criteria for Internet addiction. *CyberPsychology and Behavior*, 4, 377-383.

Correll, S. (1995). The ethnography of an electronic bar. *Journal of Contemporary Ethnography,* 24, 270-298.

Dombrowski, S. C., LeMasney, J. W., and Ahia, C. E. (2004). Protecting children from online sexual predators: Technological, psychoeducational, and legal considerations, *Professional Psychology: Research and Practice*, 35, 65-73.

Friess, S. (1998, February 3). A place where no one knows your name. *The Advocate.* 24-31.

Goolkasian, P. (1995). Psychology and its role in information technology. *Behavior Research Methods, Instruments, and Computers,* 27, 109-115.

Griffiths, M. (1997). Psychology of computer use: XLIII. Some comments on 'Addictive Use of the Internet' by Young. *Psychological Reports,* 80, 81-82.

Griffiths, M. (1998). Internet addiction: Does it really exist? In J. Gackenbach (Ed.), *Psychology and the Internet* (pp. 61-75). San Diego, CA: Academic Press.

Griffiths, M. (2001). Sex on the Internet: Observations and implications for Internet sex addiction. *Journal of Sex Research*, 38, 333-342.

Harmon, A. (1998). Researchers find sad, lonely, world in cyberspace. *New York Times.* Retrieved January 10, 2001, from http://www.nytimes.com/library/tech/98/08/ biztech/articles/30depression.html

Jaffe, J. H. (1990). Trivializing dependence. *British Journal of Addiction,* 85, 1425-1427.

Kandell, J. J. (1998). Internet addiction on campus: The vulnerability of college students. *CyberPsychology and Behavior,* 1, 11-17.

Kiesler, S., Siegel, J., and McGuire, T. W., (1984). Social psychological aspects of computer-mediated communication. *American Psychologist,* 39, 1123-1134.

King, S. A. (1996). *Is the Internet addictive, or are addicts using the Internet?* Retrieved January 9, 2002 from http://rdz.stjohns.edu/~storm/iad.html

Kraut, R., Patterson, M., Lundmark, V., Kiesler, S., Mukopadhyay, T., and Scherlis, W. (1998). Internet paradox: A social technology that reduces social involvement and psychological well-being? *American Psychologist,* 53, 1017-1031.

Lin, S. S. J. and Tsai, C. (2002). Sensation seeking and Internet dependence of Tawainese high school adolescents. *Computers in Human Behavior*, 18, 411-426.

Mariano, G. (2002). Web usage grows across globe. Retireved June 20, 2007 from http://news.com.com/2100-1023-934655.html

Marlatt, G. A. (1985). Relapse prevention: Theoretical rationale and overview of the model. In Marlatt, G. A. and Gordon, J. *Relapse Prevention.* New York, NY: The Guilford Press.

McCormick, N. B. and McCormick, J. W. (1992). Computer friends and foes: Content of undergraduates' electronic mail. *Computers in Human Behavior,* 8, 379-405.

McNamee, S. (1996). Therapy and identity construction in a post-modern world. In D. Grodin, and T. R. Lindlof (Eds.), *Constructing the self in a mediated world. Inquires in social construction.* Thousand Oaks, CA: Sage Publications, Inc.

Morahan-Martin, J. M. (1999). The relationship between loneliness and Internet use and abuse. *CyberPsychology and Behavior*, 2, 431-439.

Morahan-Martin, J. M. and Schumacher, P. (2000). Incidence and correlates of pathological Internet use among college students. *Computers in Human Behavior,* 16, 13-29.

Neilson/NetRatings (2007). U.S. average web usage month of May 2007 home panel. Retrieved June 20, 2007 from http://www.netratings.com/reports.jsp?section=pub_reportsandreport=usageandperiod=monthlyandpanel_type=2.

Oravec, J. A. (2000). Internet and computer technology hazards: Perspectives for family counseling. *British Journal of Guidance and Counseling*, 28, 309-324.

Parks, M. R., and Floyd, K. (1996). Making friends in cyberspace. *Journal of Communication,* 46, 80-97.

Peele, S., and Brodsky, A. (1991). *The Truth About Addiction and Recovery.* New York, NY: Simon and Schuster.

Pike, R., (1999). *Log on, tune in, drop out.* Retrieved January 10, 2002 from http://abcnews.go.com/sections/living/DailyNews/netaddiciton032699.html.

Pocius, K. E. (1991). Personality factors in human-computer interaction: A review of the literature. *Computers in Human Behavior*, **7**, 103-135.

Pratarelli, M. E., Browne, B. L., and Johnson, K. (1999). The bits and bytes of computer/Internet addiction: A factor analysis approach. *Behavior Research Methods, Instruments, and Computers*, 31, 305-314.

Scherer, K. (1997). College life on-line: Healthy and unhealthy Internet use. *Journal of College Student Development,* 38, 655-665.

Search Engines. (1999, July 30). *Entertainment Weekly,* 496, 81.

Shotton, M. (1989). *Computer Addiction?* New York, NY: Taylor and Francis, Inc.

Stanton, M. D., and Heath, A. W. (1997). Family and marital therapy. In J. Lowinson, P., Ruiz, R. Millman, and J. Langrod (Eds.), *Substance Abuse: A comprehensive textbook, third edition.* (pp. 448-454). Baltimore, MD: Williams and Wilkins.

Stern, S. E. (1999). Addiction to technologies: A social psychological perspective of Internet addiction. *CyberPsychology and Behavior*, 2, 419-424.

Suler, J. (1996a). *Computer and cyberspace addiction.* Retrieved January 9, 2002, from http://www1.rider.edu/~suler/psycyber/cybaddict.html

Suler, J. (1996b). *Why is this thing eating my life? Computer and cyberspace addiction at the "Palace."* Retrieved January 9, 2002 from http://www1.rider.edu/~suler/psycyber/ cybaddict.html

Treuer, T., Fabian, Z., and Furedi, J. (2001). Internet addiction associated with features of impulse control disorder: Is it a real psychiatric disorder. *Journal of Affective Disorders*, 66, 283.

Turkle, S. (1996). Parallel lives: Working on identity in virtual space. In D. Grodin, and T. R. Lindlof (Eds.), *Constructing the self in a mediated world. Inquires in social construction.* Thousand Oaks, CA: Sage Publications, Inc.

Wang, W. (2001). Internet dependency and psychosocial maturity among college students. *International Journal of Human-Computer Studies*, 55, 919-938.

Walther, J. B., and Reid, L. D. (2000). Understanding the allure of the Internet. *Chronicle of Higher Education,* B4-B5.

Winn, M. (1985). *The Plug-In Drug. New York*, N.Y.: Viking Penguin Inc.

Xuanhui, L. and Gonggu, Y. (2001). Internet addiction disorder, online behavior, and personality. *Chinese Mental Health Journal*, 15, 281-283.

Young, K. S. (1995). *Internet addiction: Symptoms, evaluation, and treatment.* Retrieved January 9, 2002, from http://www.netaddiction.com/articles/ symptoms.html

Young, K. S. (1996b). *Internet addiction: The emergence of a new clinical disorder.* Retrieved January 9, 2002, from http://www.netaddiction.com/ articles/newdisorder.html.

Young, K. S. (1997). *What makes the Internet addictive: Potential explanations for pathological Internet use.* Retrieved October 25, 2001, from http://www.netaddiction.com/articles/hatbitforming.html.

Young, K. S. (1998a). *The center for on-line addiction - Frequently asked questions.* Retrieved January 9, 2002, from http://www.netaddiction. com/resources/faq.html.

Young, K. S. (1998b). *Caught in the Net.* New York, NY: John Wiley and Sons, Inc.

Young, K. S., Pistner, M., and O'Mara, J. (1999). *Cyber disorders: The mental health concern for the new millennium. CyberPsychology and Behavior*, 2, 475-479.

INDEX

C

D

I

J

K

L

M

N

O

P

Q

R

S

T

U

V

W

Y